I CHING

SHAMBHALA POCKET CLASSICS

THE ART OF PEACE:
Teachings of the Founder of Aikido
by Morihei Ueshiba
Compiled and translated by John Stevens

THE ART OF WAR by Sun Tzu
Translated by Thomas Cleary

THE ART OF WORLDLY WISDOM
by Balthasar Gracián

BACK TO BEGINNINGS by Huanchu Daoren
Translated by Thomas Cleary

THE BOOK OF FIVE RINGS by Miyamoto Musas
Translated by Thomas Cleary

THE BOOK OF TEA by Kakuzo Okakura

COLD MOUNTAIN: 101 Chinese Poems
by Han-shan
Translated by Burton Watson

DHAMMAPADA: The Sayings of the Buddha
Rendered by Thomas Byrom

For a complete list, send for our catalogue:
Shambhala Publications
P.O. Box 308
Boston, MA 02117-0308

I CHING

The Book of Change

A complete & unabridged
translation by
THOMAS CLEARY

SHAMBHALA

Boston & London

1992

Shambhala Publications, Inc.
Horticultural Hall
300 Massachusetts Avenue
Boston, Massachusetts 02115
http://www.shambhala.com

9 8 7 6

Printed in Singapore
♾ This edition is printed on acid-free paper that meets the
American National Standards Institute Z39.48 Standard.
Distributed in the United States by
Random House, Inc., in Canada by
Random House of Canada Ltd.

See p. 170 for CIP data.

CONTENTS

INTRODUCTION

The Book of Change is the most ancient and most profound of the Chinese classics, venerated for millennia as an oracle of fortune, a guide to success, and a dispensary of wisdom. The ancestor of all Chinese philosophy, it is the primary source for the pragmatic mysticism of the *Tao Te Ching,* the rational humanism of Confucius, and the analytic strategy of Sun Tzu's *Art of War.*

The Book of Change was originally composed over three thousand years ago by a king and his son in the tutelage of a Taoist sage. Six centuries later, the book was analyzed and annotated by Confucius, the great scholar and educator. The result of this work was the classic in the format known today, a compendium of advice on the causes behind the rise and fall of kingdoms and careers.

The earliest function of the core symbols of *The Book of Change* is traditionally said to have been as a system of notation, a tool for grouping associations and defining relations symbolically. This system evolved into a language of logic for describing the courses of actions and events.

The sources of *The Book of Change* lore are thus to be found in the origins of writing itself, in the attempt to depict phenomena and events in written symbols. The structures of *The Book of Change* represent dynamic patterns of causal relations; the total design of the book constitutes a symbolic language generating descriptions of relationships as they change over time.

The original recorded versions of *The Book of Change* would have been inscribed on strips of bamboo or wood, which when arrayed for the purposes of consultation would not resemble a modern book in form or structure. The internal order was maintained by the relationships among the principal symbols, which by virtue of their complexity allowed several different systems of interrelation to coexist within the internal order of the abstract *Book of Change*.

Consulting
THE BOOK OF CHANGE

A convenient method of consulting the book is given in an ancient appendix attributed to Confucius, according to the following directions:

Change has an absolute limit:
This produces two modes;
The two modes produce four forms,
The four forms produce eight
    trigrams;
The eight trigrams determine fortune
    and misfortune.

This formula summarizes the basis of the structure of *The Book of Change,* from which is derived the simplest method of drawing specific advice from the book.

1. The "absolute limit" of change refers to mental quietude. The first step in consulting *The Book of Change* is to calm the mind.

2. The "two modes" are yin and yang. These abstract terms stand for flexibility and firmness, weakness and strength, stillness and movement, passivity and activity, sadness and happiness, depression and elation.

Identification of yin and yang factors and qualities in a person or situation helps the reader to understand and apply the statements on the yin/yang components of each sign of *The Book of Change*.

Note that yin and yang do not symbolize femininity and masculinity in *The Book of Change*. In the symbolism of this system, a female represents yin and a male represents yang, but not the other way around.

A female symbol therefore does not represent female gender, and a male symbol does not represent male gender; yin does not represent women and yang does not represent men. Yin and yang are universal complements that occur in all people and events.

It is also important to note that yin and yang do not symbolize bad and good. Yin and yang can be either good or bad, according to the function of the quality in a given situation.

3. The "four forms" are called major and minor yin and yang. The yin mode is subdivided into major yin and minor yang, or climaxing yin and incipient yang. The yang mode is subdivided into major yang and minor yin, or climaxing yang and incipient yin.

The significance of these subdivisions is in representation of the principle that yin and yang modes are not static, but are always in the process of waxing or waning.

4. The "eight trigrams" produced by the four forms of yin and yang complete the foundation of the book, and finally yield the symbols used to manipulate the book for spot consultation:

Major yang trigrams: SKY and LAKE
Minor yin trigrams: THUNDER and FIRE
Major yin trigrams: EARTH and MOUNTAIN
Minor yang trigrams: WATER and WIND

The permutations of these eight symbols form the cores of the sixty-four chapters of *The Book of Change*. Accordingly, the consultation is carried out through the juxtaposition of their symbolic values:

SKY represents *strength* or *creativity*.
LAKE represents *joy* or *attraction*.
THUNDER represents *initiative* or *action*.
FIRE represents *attention* or *awareness*.
EARTH represents *receptivity* or *docility*.
MOUNTAIN represents *stopping* or *stillness*.
WATER represents *passion* or *danger*.
WIND represents *penetrating* or *following*.

The consultation is done by selecting a pair of symbols representing qualities relevant to the situation under consideration. These may stand for facets of personality and character in individual people or groups, or for dominant forces in the fabric of an event, activity, or undertaking.

Each pair of symbols produces two hexagrams (or one, where the same symbol is taken twice). These become the text for consultation, reading in the manner described below. Please refer to the charts at the end of this introduction for the combinations of trigrams, the hexagrams they produce, and examples of typical relationships and situations they may be used to represent.

Once the hexagrams have been selected, their specific application to the subject of interest is a personal matter, it being the nature of *The Book of Change* to vary in meaning according to many individual factors, including the mood and personality of the reader. For enhanced perspective on a given reading, moreover, each hexagram may also be paired with two others, a primal correlate and a structural complement. (In a few cases the primal correlate and structural complement are the same.) See the back of the book for a list of the hexagrams with their correlates and complements.

In actual practice, furthermore, interpreters of the book have traditionally *always* read it *as a whole system* and made their explanations in light of awareness of the total philosophy. It is the overall integrity and coherence of the book that underlie its efficacy; thus it is traditionally considered advisable to read the book in its entirety in order to maximize its benefits.

THE BOOK OF CHANGE
Readings

The first element of an individual reading is the title of the hexagram, which suggests a certain theme, consisting of an archetypal element or aspect of human life. This is followed by a summary statement of pragmatic philosophy relative to that theme.

The next element of the reading is the "overall judgment," Confucius's analysis of the theme and statement, elaborating the relationships of the elements represented by the trigrams. This is followed by an aphorism, also attributed to Confucius, based on the imagery of the hexagram as a pair of specific trigrams.

The theme, statement, overall judgment, and imagery aphorism form the abstract core of each chapter and are the parts that are read when the classic is consulted for general knowledge or perused at leisure in the ordinary course of events.

The following statements on the components, which deal with specific ways of handling oneself in situations of relative strength and weakness, are also read when the consultation deals with unexpected or unpredictable changes. As a consequence of their frame of reference, the relevance of the components may be to past, future, or other factors outside the immediate present.

Reference to the primal correlate and the structural complement of the hexagram in question enlarges the perspective and adds depth and dimension to the reflection fostered by the reading.

CONSULTATION CHART

TRIGRAMS UPPER → LOWER ↓	Sky	Lake	Thunder	Fire	Earth	Mountain	Water	Wind
Sky	1	43	34	14	11	26	5	9
Lake	10	58	54	38	19	41	60	61
Thunder	25	17	51	21	24	27	3	42
Fire	13	49	55	30	36	22	63	37
Earth	12	45	16	35	2	23	8	20
Mountain	33	31	62	56	15	52	39	53
Water	6	47	40	64	7	4	29	59
Wind	44	28	32	50	46	18	48	57

Key

> SKY: *strength/creativity*
> LAKE: *joy/attraction*
> THUNDER: *initiative/action*
> FIRE: *attention/awareness*
> EARTH: *receptivity/docility*
> MOUNTAIN: *stopping/stillness*
> WATER: *passion/danger*
> WIND: *penetrating/following*

Examples

1. A relationship between someone who is very intelligent and someone who is very adaptable might be represented by a combination of fire and wind. Fire over wind yields hexagram number 50, THE CAULDRON. Wind over fire yields number 37, PEOPLE IN THE HOME.

2. A situation in which one faction is eager to move ahead in an undertaking while another faction is hesitant and inhibited might be represented by a combination of thunder and mountain. Thunder over mountain yields number 62, PREDOMI-

NANCE OF THE SMALL. Mountain over thunder yields number 27, NOURISHMENT.

3. If you tend to be lighthearted but are in perilous circumstances, this might be represented by a combination of lake and water. Lake over water yields number 47, EXHAUSTION. Water over lake yields number 60, REGULATION.

The Book of Change

1. THE CREATIVE

Great success benefits the upright and true.

OVERALL JUDGMENT

Vast indeed is the scope of the greatness of the creative basis. All things and all beings originate from it, so it sums up the totality of Nature.

Like clouds raining as they go, things and beings flow in forms. When you have an overall understanding of their processes, how they begin and end, when the six stages have been accomplished in a timely manner, then you ride the six dragons to harness Nature.

The evolutionary developments of the Way of the Creative each straighten out essential life and preserve overall harmony intact. This is what benefits the upright and true. When it emerges to lead the people, all countries are peaceful.

IMAGE

The action of Nature is powerful; cultured

people use it to strengthen themselves cease-
lessly.

COMPONENTS

1 *yang*. Do not use the hidden dragon. *Image.*
Do not use the hidden dragon when positive
energy is low.

2 *yang*. When you see the dragon in the field,
it is worthwhile to see great people. *Image.*
When you see the dragon in the field, it
means that the use of your inner character,
qualities, and powers affects everything you
do.

3 *yang*. If cultivated people work diligently
all day and are serious at night, then they
will not err in dangerous situations. *Image.*
Working diligently means going over and
over the Way.

4 *yang*. One may leap at times in the deep,
with no fault. *Image.* One may leap at times
in the depths insofar as there have been no
mistakes in the process of development.

5 *yang*. When the flying dragons are in the
sky, it is worthwhile seeing great people. *Im-*

age. When flying dragons are in the sky is when great people are working creatively.

6 yang. Dragons that fly too high have regrets. *Image.* Dragons that fly too high have regrets; this means that fullness cannot last forever.

Using Yang. When you see a group of dragons with no head, it is lucky. *Image.* In using yang, celestial qualities cannot be deliberately made to be in the forefront.

 ## 2. THE RECEPTIVE

Great success beneficial to a chaste mare. Cultured people have places to go; if they get lost first, it is to their advantage to find a leader later on. With yin companions and no yang companions, there is peace; it bodes well to be steadfast and true.

OVERALL JUDGMENT

Perfect indeed is the greatness of the receptive earth, which sustains the birth of all beings and accords with what it receives from heaven.

The richness of earth supports beings, its virtue is one with the unbounded, it contains within it vast glory and magnificence, through which all things and beings successfully exist.

The mare is akin to the earth, traveling the earth without bound, gentle and docile, helpful and faithful. Cultured people are going somewhere: earlier they got lost and strayed from the Way, later they followed and attained the eternal.

Having yin companions is going with peers; having no yang companions means joy is in the end. The good omen of stability and steadfastness corrresponds to the boundlessness of earth.

IMAGE

The attitude of earth is receptive. Cultured people support others by enriching character.

COMPONENTS

1 *yin.* Walking on frost, you come to solid ice. *Image.* Walking on frost and solid ice stand for the initial congealing of yin. Follow

that path all the way, and you come to solid ice.

2 *yin.* Being honest, straight, and magnanimous will help everything, even without practice. *Image.* The action of balanced yin is honest and straight. It helps everything, even without practice, because the Way of earth is enlightening.

3 *yin.* Hide your adornments; it is well to be chaste. If you work in government, you do not do anything, but you get things done. *Image.* Hiding your adornments and being chaste mean going into action only at the right time. If you work in service of the affairs of leadership, your knowledge is illuminated and expanded.

4 *yin.* Shut the bag, and there is neither blame nor praise. *Image.* Shutting the bag so there is no blame is being careful to avoid harm.

5 *yin.* A yellow garment is very auspicious. *Image.* To say that a yellow garment is very auspicious means that culture is centered.

6 *yin.* When dragons battle in the fields, their blood is dusky yellow. *Image.* Dragons battling in the fields means the way has come to an end.

Using Yin. It is benefitial to always be steadfast and true. *Image.* When using yin, always be steadfast and true in order to arrive at a great conclusion.

 3. DIFFICULTY

Great success is beneficial for the honest. Do not deliberately hold to a specific goal. It is useful to establish local leaders.

OVERALL JUDGMENT

In difficulty, firmness and flexibility begin to interact, and problems arise. Acting right in the middle of dangerous straits, great success comes through for the honest and true. As thunder and rain fill the body, Nature creates confusion and darkness. It is useful to establish local leaders, but it is not peaceful.

IMAGE

Clouds and thunder make difficulty; thus cultured people consider reasons.

COMPONENTS

1 *yang.* When you are hesitant and not getting anywhere, it is advantageous to remain upright. It is useful to set up local leaders. *Image.* Even though you are not getting anywhere, your intentions and actions are to be correct. By respecting the lowly, many people are won.

2 *yin.* Stopped, not getting anywhere, mounted on a horse but at a standstill, do not be hostile, but form a partnership. A girl is chaste; she does not get engaged. After ten years she becomes engaged. *Image.* What is difficult for the weak and pliable to do here is to ride upon the strong and adamant. Becoming engaged after ten years means returning to normalcy.

3 *yin.* Chase deer without a guide, and you will only go into the forest. Cultured people sense that it is better to give up and that it would be regrettable to go. *Image.* Chasing

deer without a guide means following the wild animals. Cultured people give up on this, since to go on would bring regret, because it would be fruitless.

4 *yin*. Mounted on a horse, yet at a standstill, if you seek partnership it bodes well to go ahead; there is no disadvantage. *Image*. It is intelligent to go seeking.

5 *yang*. When stalling the benefits, a little steadfastness is auspicious, a lot of steadfastness is unlucky. *Image*. Stalling the benefits means that the giving forth is not yet carried out on a large scale.

6 *yin*. Mounted on a horse but at a standstill, you weep tears of blood. *Image*. You weep tears of blood, for what can last?

4. INNOCENCE

Innocence gets through successfully. Though you do not seek the innocent yourself, the innocent seek you. The first augury informs, the second and third muddle. Muddling is not informative. It is advantageous to be correct.

OVERALL JUDGMENT

In innocence, there is danger below a mountain. Stopping at danger is innocence. Innocence gets through by successful action at the right time. Though you do not seek the innocent yourself, the innocent seek you, because your aspirations correspond. The first augury informs, because of being firmly on target. The second and third muddle, and muddling is not informative, because it muddles innocence. To take advantage of innocence to nurture honesty is the work of sages.

IMAGE

A spring emerging under a mountain stands for innocence. Cultured people nurture character by fruitful action.

COMPONENTS

1 *yin.* It is advantageous to use punishments to awaken the ignorant; it is regrettable to go on without restrictions. *Image.* It is advantageous to use punishments, if it is done through just laws.

2 *yang.* It is auspicious to embrace the inno- cent. It is auspicious to take a wife. The off- spring takes over as head of the family. *Im- age.* The offspring taking over as head of the family represents the conjoining of firmness and flexibility.

3 *yin.* Do not take a girl to see a rich man, for if she is not self-possessed there is no benefit. *Image.* Do not take a partner who is incompatible.

4 *yin.* It is regrettable to be thwarted by ig- norance. *Image.* The shame of being thwarted by ignorance is having strayed from reality by yourself.

5 *yin.* Innocence is auspicious. *Image.* What is auspicious about innocence is harmonizing smoothly.

6 *yang.* Attacking ignorance, it is not benefi- cial to be a brigand, it is beneficial to ward off brigands. *Image.* It is advantageous to de- liberately ward off brigands; those on top and those below agree.

5. WAITING

When waiting is truthful, it is gloriously successful; be truthfully steadfast, and you will be lucky. It is profitable to cross great rivers.

OVERALL JUDGMENT

Waiting is necessary; when danger lies ahead, that is. When strength is robust and not trapped, its justice is not thwarted and its duty is not frustrated. When waiting is truthful, it is gloriously successful; be truthfully steadfast, and you will be lucky; this means you will take your place in the order of Nature by way of correct balance. That it is profitable to cross great rivers means that progressive action will accomplish something.

IMAGE

Clouds ascend to the heavens, waiting; thus do cultured people relax and enjoy food and drink.

COMPONENTS

1 *yang.* Waiting on the outskirts, it is worthwhile to try to be constant, so that you may be faultless. *Image.* Waiting on the outskirts means not having gotten into difficult and problematic activities. It is worthwhile to try to be constant, so that you may be faultless; this is assuming that you have not already become abnormal.

2 *yang.* Waiting on sand is criticized a little, but there is a good ending. *Image.* Waiting on sand means there is an abundance in the center. Although there is a little criticism, it can be used to make the end felicitous.

3 *yang.* Waiting in mud brings on emenies. *Image.* Waiting in mud means there is trouble outside. Once you have brought enemies on yourself, be serious and careful not to get beaten.

4 *yin.* Waiting in blood, come out from your own cave. *Image.* Waiting in blood means listening obediently.

5 *yang.* Waiting with wine and food, it bodes well to be steadfast and true. *Image.* With

wine and food, it is good to be chaste; that means being balanced and proper.

6 *yin.* Going into a cave, there are three unhurried guests coming. Respect them, and you will eventually have good luck. *Image.* When three unhurried guests come, be respectful to them, and you will be lucky in the end. Even if you do not attain status or position, you will not have lost much.

6. CONTENTION

Contention means there is obstruction of truth; be wary. Balance bodes well, finality bodes ill. It is worthwhile to see great people, but not worthwhile to cross great rivers.

OVERALL JUDGMENT

Contention is adamant above and dangerous below, representing powerful contention in danger. Contention means there is obstruction of truth; be careful to remain centered and balanced, and you will have good luck. This refers to strength emerging in balance. Finality bodes ill, because contention cannot be made to conclude. It is worthwhile to see great people, in the sense of valuing balance and rectitude. It is not worthwhile to cross great rivers, because you would plunge into an abyss.

IMAGE

Sky and water going in different directions symbolize contention. Thus do cultured people calculate and plan how to begin whenever they do things.

COMPONENTS

1 *yin.* If you do not persist forever in an affair, there may be some talk, but all will be well in the end. *Image.* Not persisting forever in an affair means that contention is not to be prolonged. Although there may be some talk, there will be clarification.

2 *yang.* If you do not win your suit, go home and hide. With three hundred families in your hometown, there will be no trouble. *Image.* If you do not win your suit, go home and hide to get out of harm's way. When suits are brought against those above by

those below, problems come up that must be taken on.

3 *yin.* Though living on past merits, if you are steadfast and diligent you will eventually be lucky. If you pursue government work, you do not make anything happen. *Image.* Living on past merits is the luck of following the ascendant order.

4 *yang.* If you do not win your suit, go back and take to your fate, change over to peace. It bodes well to be steadfast. *Image.* Going back to take to your fate, changing to become peaceful, it bodes well to be steadfast; this means not slipping.

5 *yang.* Contention may be very lucky. *Image.* Contention is very lucky when it is balanced and correct.

6 *yang.* You may be presented with a belt of honor, but it will be taken away from you three times before the day is out. *Image.* Even if one receives acknowledgment of victory through contention, that does not mean one is worthy of respect.

7. AN ARMY

If an army is to be upright, it is auspicious to have mature people; then there is no blame.

OVERALL JUDGMENT

An army is a group; to be upright is to be correct. Those who are able to employ groups correctly can thereby become leaders. When strength is centered it is responsive; action in dangerous straits is obedient. Even if this poisons the world, the people will follow it. If there is good luck, what blame will there be?

IMAGE

Within the earth there is water, an army; thus do leaders take people in and care for the masses.

COMPONENTS

1 *yin.* An army is to go forth in an orderly manner; if not, there will be misfortune even if there is a good cause. *Image.* An army is to go forth in an orderly manner because it will have bad luck if it loses order.

2 *yang.* In the middle of the army, if there is good luck there is no blame. The leader gives out directives three times. *Image.* Being lucky in the middle of the army means receiving the favor of Nature. The leader giving out directives three times symbolizes concern for all nations.

3 *yin.* An army may sustain casualties, which is inauspicious. *Image.* If an army sustains casualties, that is a great failure.

4 *yin.* When an army camps at a distance, there is no trouble. *Image.* When an army camps at a distance there is no trouble, since things are still normal.

5 *yin.* When there are vermin in the fields, it is profitable to catch and denounce them; then there is no error. Mature people should lead the expedition; the immature would sustain casualties even if they were upright and steadfast. *Image.* Mature people lead an army with balanced action; immature people sustain casualties because they are not up to their mission.

6 *yin.* A great leader has directives to found

states and perpetuate families. Petty people are not to be elected. *Image.* Great leaders have directives by virtue of just success. Petty people are not to be elected, because they are sure to disturb the state.

 8. ACCORD

Accord is auspicious. If the basis of the augury is always right, there is no error. The unsettled will then come; stragglers will be unlucky.

OVERALL JUDGMENT

Accord is auspicious, for accord means helping, humbly following along in harmony. If the basis of the augury is always right, there is no error; this refers to firm strength in centered balance. The uneasy will then come, for there is response between those above and those below. Stragglers will be unlucky, for they will come to an impasse.

IMAGE

Upon the earth is water, symbolizing accord; thus did ancient kings set up a multitude of states and associate with their leaders.

COMPONENTS

1 *yin.* Accord with the truthful is blameless. When truthfulness fills a plain vessel, eventually it brings other good fortune. *Image.* Flexibility in the helping of accord will have other good fortune.

2 *yin.* Accord that comes from inner rectitude bodes well. *Image.* That accord comes from within means that you do not lose yourself.

3 *yin.* There is accord with the wrong people. *Image.* If there is accord with the wrong people, is that not harmful?

4 *yin.* Correctness in accord with those outside bodes well. *Image.* Accord with the wise outside, so as to follow their progress.

5 *yang.* Make accord evident. A king uses three chasers, overlooking the game in front. When the local people are not wary, that bodes well. *Image.* Making accord evident means taking one's place right in the center. Giving up on the obstreperous and taking in the harmonious is symbolized by overlooking the game in front. When the local people are

not wary, that means the rulership has brought about balance.

6 *yin.* Accord without direction is unlucky. *Image.* Accord without direction never finishes anything.

9. NURTURE OF THE SMALL

Nurture of the small is successful. Dense clouds not raining come from your own western region.

OVERALL JUDGMENT

Nurture of the small means that flexibility gains status, and above and below respond to it. Powerful yet docile, with strength in balance, your aim is carried out, and thus you succeed. Dense clouds not raining means still being on the move; coming from your own western region means practical measures have yet to be executed.

IMAGE

Wind traveling up in the sky symbolizes nurture of the small; thus do leaders beautify the qualities of their culture.

COMPONENTS

1 *yang.* If you return by the Way, what is the problem? This is auspicious. *Image.* When you return by the Way, it is auspicious that you act rightly.

2 *yang.* Leading back is auspicious. *Image.* Leading back to central balance, you do not lose yourself.

3 *yang.* A cart has its wheels removed, husband and wife look away from each other. *Image.* Husband and wife looking away from each other cannot make a home properly.

4 *yin.* When there is sincerity, bloodiness goes and fear departs, so there is no trouble. *Image.* When there is sincerity, fear departs, because there is agreement higher up.

5 *yang.* When there is sincerity, it forms links, enriching the neighborhood. *Image.* When there is sincerity it forms links, not enjoying riches alone.

6 *yang.* It has rained and settled, and lofty attainment has built up; the wife is chaste

and diligent. The moon almost full, it is in-auspicious for a leader to go on an expedition. *Image.* Having rained and settled represents fullness of attainment. It is inauspicious for a leader to go on an expedition when there is something in doubt.

10. TREADING

To tread on a tiger's tail without getting bitten by the tiger, to get through successfully it is advantageous to be steady.

OVERALL JUDGMENT

Treading means flexibility treading on hardness. It is joyful response to the creativity of heaven, so one can tread on a tiger's tail without the tiger's biting, getting through successfully. With firm strength balanced correctly, if one can tread the way of leadership without ailing, that is illumined.

IMAGE

Sky above with lake below symbolize treading; thus do leaders distinguish above and below and define the aspirations of the people.

COMPONENTS

1 *yang.* Treading with basics, there is nothing wrong in proceeding. *Image.* Proceeding to tread with basics means carrying out vows alone.

2 *yang.* Treading the road, it is level; a person in obscurity is lucky if steadfast and upright. *Image.* A person in obscurity is lucky if steadfast and upright; this means being centered and not becoming wild.

3 *yin.* Seeing squint-eyed, walking with a limp, when treading on a tiger's tail you get bitten, to your misfortune. A soldier becomes a major leader. *Image.* Seeing squint-eyed means you cannot see clearly; walking with a limp means you cannot get along. The misfortune of getting bitten is being in a position that you cannot fulfill properly. For a soldier to become a major leader means that the will is firm.

4 *yang.* Treading on a tiger's tail, be very cautious and it will turn out all right. *Image.*

Extreme caution that turns out all right is deliberate action.

5 *yang.* Decisive treading means steadfast diligence. *Image.* Decisive treading means steadfast diligence; this is when you manage your position correctly.

6 *yang.* With observant treading, examine details carefully, and the return will be very auspicious. *Image.* There is major celebration when great good fortune comes to the leadership.

11. TRANQUILLITY

With tranquillity, the small goes and the great comes, with auspicious success.

OVERALL JUDGMENT

With tranquillity, the small goes and the great comes, with auspicious success: this means heaven and earth interact, so that all things and beings attain fulfillment. Above and below interact, and their wills are the same. Yang inside and yin outside symbolize inward strength with outward docility, being a cultivated person within while appearing outwardly to be an ordinary person. The ways of cultivated people go on and on, the ways of ordinary people disappear.

IMAGE

Heaven and earth interacting is tranquillity. Thus do leaders administer the ways of heaven and earth, assisting the balance of heaven and earth to help the people.

COMPONENTS

1 *yang*. Pull out a reed, and it brings others of its kind with it. An expedition will be lucky. *Image.* Pulling out a reed and the luck of an expedition refer to the will being set outside.

2 *yang*. Embrace the desolate, employ those who can cross rivers, do not neglect those far away; when partisanship is gone, you can discover the value of balanced action. *Image.* Embracing the desolate and getting the value of balanced action are means of glory and greatness.

3 *yang*. There is no level without incline, no going without return. In hardship and diffi-

culty, the steadfast and true are blameless; let them not grieve over their sincerity, for they will have plenty to eat. *Image.* There is no level without incline; this is the border of sky and earth.

4 *yin.* The flighty do not prosper as those around them do. They are not careful about being truthful. *Image.* Being flighty and not prospering both refer to lack of substantiality and fulfillment. Not being careful about truthfulness refers to inner wishes.

5 *yin.* The emperor marries off his younger sister for good luck, and it is very auspicious. *Image.* To act for good luck and have it be very auspicious means to act on aspirations in a balanced way.

6 *yin.* When the citadel walls crumble into the moat, do not deploy the army. Trying to promulgate order from your own hometown is shameful even if it is right. *Image.* The citadel walls crumbling into the moat represent the disruption of order.

12. OBSTRUCTION

The inhumanity of obstruction does not help the steadfast uprightness of cultured people. The great goes and the small comes.

OVERALL JUDGMENT

The inhumanity of obstruction does not profit cultured people who are steadfast and upright; the great goes and the small comes. This means that when heaven and earth do not interact, things and beings do not attain fulfillment. When above and below do not interact, no country in the world can survive. Having yin inside and yang outside symbolizes being inwardly weak but outwardly adamant, being an ordinary person inside while putting on the outward appearance of being a cultured person; thus the ways of ordinary people go on and on, while the ways of cultured people disappear.

IMAGE

Heaven and earth not interacting symbolizes obstruction; under such conditions cultured

people avoid trouble by virtue of frugality,
unwilling to work just for money.

COMPONENTS

1 *yin.* Pull out a reed, and it brings along
others of its kind. Correctness means luck
and success. *Image.* When a reed is pulled
out, correctness brings good luck, because
the aim is up to the leader.

2 *yin.* Embracing service is lucky for ordinary
people but an obstruction for great people;
yet they get through successfully. *Image.*
When great people are obstructed yet do get
through successfully, they do not disturb the
crowd.

3 *yin.* It is shameful to be taken in. *Image.*
The shame of being taken in is being put in
an inappropriate position.

4 *yang.* When there is order, there is no
fault; companions cleave to blessings. *Image.*
When there is order, there is no fault; the
aim is carried out.

5 *yang.* Stopping obstruction, great people
are lucky; still keeping destruction in mind,

they persist in holding to means of sustenance. *Image.* The luck of great people is being in the appropriate position.

6 *yang.* Overthrowing obstruction, first there is obstruction, afterward there is joy. *Image.* When obstruction ends, it collapses; what can last?

13. SAMENESS WITH PEOPLE

Sameness with people in the wilds is successful. It is worthwhile crossing great rivers. It is worthwhile to be upright as cultured people.

OVERALL JUDGMENT

In sameness with people, flexibility finds its place and attains balance, thus responding to the creative. This is called sameness with people. When it says that sameness with people in the wild is successful, and that it is worthwhile to cross great rivers, this refers to creative activity. Civilization is responsive when its strength is balanced and upright;

this is the rectitude of cultured people. Only cultured people can understand the mentalities of the whole world.

IMAGE

Sky and fire symbolize sameness with people. Thus do cultured people distinguish things and beings in terms of types and kinds.

COMPONENTS

1 *yang*. Be the same as people at the gate, and there will be no blame. *Image.* And who would blame you if you were the same as people beyond the gate?

2 *yin*. Being the same as people in a clannish way leads to regret. *Image.* Assimilation to others in a clannish way is a route to shame.

3 *yang*. Hiding warriors in the bush, climbing to a high outlook, do not take action for three years. *Image.* Hiding warriors in the bush refers to a situation where there is strong opposition. Not taking action for three years means acting calmly.

4 *yang*. When you climb the walls but cannot attack successfully, that is lucky. *Image.*

When you climb the walls, it is right that you do not succeed. The lucky thing about it is when you get frustrated and return to normal.

5 *yang.* Being the same with people, first you weep, later you laugh: the great general conquers, then holds meetings. *Image.* In the forefront of sameness with others, you use balanced honesty; when this "great general" holds meetings, what it says prevails.

6 *yang.* One can be the same as people on the outskirts without regret. *Image.* Being the same as people on the outskirts refers to times when you have not yet attained your aim.

14. GREAT POSSESSION

Great possession means great success.

OVERALL JUDGMENT

In great possession, flexibility has the important position. Greatness is balanced, with above and below responsive to it. This is called great possession. The appropriate virtues are firm strength and cultured intelligence, acting in season in accord with nature; this is the reason for great success.

IMAGE

Fire up in the sky symbolizes great possession. Cultured people in this situation stop evil and promote good, obeying heaven and accepting its order.

COMPONENTS

1 *yang.* Do not get involved with what is harmful, and you will be blameless. You will be blameless if you struggle. *Image.* Great possession is positive at first; there is no involvement with what is harmful.

2 *yang.* If you use a large car for transport and have somewhere to go, there is no mistake. *Image.* To use a large car for transport means that the load is centered, so there is no slipup.

3 *yang.* Work for the public welfare gets through to the ruler. Petty people cannot manage. *Image.* Work in the public interest

gets through to the ruler. Petty people are harmful.

4 *yang.* There is nothing wrong with repudiating whatever is imbalanced and not straighforward. *Image.* Faultlessly repudiating imbalance and crookedness means intelligently defining and analyzing them.

5 *yin.* The trust that is mutual and imbued with dignity is auspicious. *Image.* The trust that is mutual means that people can frankly reveal what is on their minds. The auspicious kind of dignity is easy and unguarded.

6 *yang.* The luck that comes from heaven's help could be beneficial to all. *Image.* The superior luck of great possession comes from heaven's help.

15. HUMILITY

Humility is successful. Cultured people have a conclusion.

OVERALL JUDGMENT

Humility is successful; the way of heaven is to help those below and shine with light.

The way of earth is to move upward from lowliness. The way of heaven lessens satiety and gives more to the humble; the way of earth shifts from satiety and flows to the humble. Ghosts and spirits hurt the satiated and bless the humble. The way of humans is to dislike the satiated and like the humble. Humility is noble and even glorious; though lowly, one cannot be surpassed. This is the conclusion of cultured people.

IMAGE

There are mountains in the earth, symbolizing humility. Cultured people take from those who have too much, to give to those who have too little, thus assessing people to deal with them impartially.

COMPONENTS

1 yin. If humbly humble cultured people use this to cross great rivers, they will be lucky. *Image.* When humbly humble cultured people are lowly, they use this to master themselves.

2 yin. Expressing humility is auspicious if it is true. *Image.* Expressing humility is auspi-

cious if it is true, in the sense of actually being there in the heart.

3 *yang*. Cultured people who work hard yet are humble have good luck in the end. *Image.* All people would follow cultured people who work hard yet are humble.

4 *yin*. In no case is it not beneficial to disperse humility. *Image.* In no case is it not beneficial to disperse humility, in the sense of not violating norms.

5 *yin*. When not prospering with the neighbors, it is advantageous to invade; all will profit. *Image.* It is advantageous to invade, in the sense of overcoming malcontent.

6 *yin*. When expressing humility, it is advantageous to deploy an army to overrun cities and states. *Image.* When one is expressing humility, that means one's aim has not yet been attained; one might use a military operation to overrun cities and states.

16. HAPPINESS

If it is for happiness, it is beneficial to set up local leaders and mobilize armies.

OVERALL JUDGMENT

In happiness, strength is responsive and aims are carried out. Acting in a harmonious way means happiness. Since happiness is acting harmoniously, even heaven and earth are like this, to say nothing of setting up local leaders and mobilizing armies. Because heaven and earth act harmoniously, the sun and moon do not go off course and the four seasons do not go out of order. As sages act harmoniously, punishments are clear and people are obedient. The meaning of the times of happiness is far reaching indeed.

IMAGE

Thunder emerging and earth stirring symbolize happiness. Thus did past leaders make music to honor virtue, abundantly offering it to God, to share with their ancestors.

COMPONENTS

1 *yin*. It is unlucky to sound off about hap-

piness. *Image.* Weak at first, if you sound off about happiness, you will be unlucky when your will is thwarted.

2 *yin.* Firm as a rock, not taking all day, be true and you will be lucky. *Image.* Not taking all day, be true and you will be lucky, to the extent that you are balanced correctly.

3 *yin.* If you look up expecting happiness, you will regret it. If you are too late, you will regret it. *Image.* To have regret because of looking up expecting happiness means to be in a position you cannot manage properly.

4 *yang.* Being a source of joy, there is great gain; do not doubt that companions will gather. *Image.* Being a source of joy and having great gain mean fully carrying out an aim.

5 *yin.* Be steadfast when ailing, and you last without dying. *Image.* Here, being steadfast when ailing means riding on strength; lasting without dying means balance has not been lost.

6 *yin.* Oblivious happiness undergoes change once it has taken place; it is nobody's fault.

Image. Oblivious happiness is at the climax; what can last?

17. FOLLOWING

Following is a great success, worthwhile if correct; then there is no fault.

OVERALL JUDGMENT

In following, firmness comes under flexibility, joyfully following its activity. If great success is correct, there is no fault, and the world follows the seasons. The meaning of following the seasons is great indeed.

IMAGE

There is thunder in a lake, symbolizing following; thus do cultured people go in and rest at sundown.

COMPONENTS

1 *yang.* When there are changes in duties, it is auspicious if they are correct. Relationships outside the gate have merit. *Image.* When there are changes in duties, it is auspicious to go along with what is right. When relationships outside the gate have merit, that means not slipping up.

2 *yin.* Getting involved with a child, you lose an adult. *Image.* Getting involved with a child means you are not with both adult and child at once.

3 *yin.* Getting involved with an adult, you lose a child. When following with a quest to gain, it is beneficial to remain steadfast. *Image.* To get involved with an adult means to set your heart on leaving lowliness behind.

4 *yang.* If you follow with acquisitiveness, you will be unlucky even if steadfast. If you have sincerity and stay on the Way by clarity, what problem is there? *Image.* To follow with acquisitiveness is unlucky by its very sense. Having sincerity and staying on the Way are achievements of clarity.

5 *yang.* Sincerity in good is auspicious. *Image.* Sincerity in good is auspicious; this means the position is correctly centered.

6 *yin.* If you are constrained by ties with something, you go along bound up with it. A king makes sacrifices. *Image.* To be constrained by ties with something means you can go no higher.

18. DISRUPTION

Disruption leads to great success. It is worthwhile crossing great rivers. Three days before, three days after.

OVERALL JUDGMENT

In disruption, there is hardness above and softness below, a flow of wind being stopped and disrupted. When disruption leads to great success, the world is pacified. It is beneficial to cross great rivers, in the sense that there is purpose in your actions. Three days before and three days after refer to creative action, which begins again after it finishes.

IMAGE

There is wind under a mountain, disrupted. Cultured people inspire others to develop virtue.

COMPONENTS

1 *yin.* If there is a son dealing with the disruption of the father, there is no blame on the late father. If he is diligent, there will be

good luck in the end. *Image.* Dealing with the disruption of the father means intending to take up after the late father.

2 *yang.* Dealing with the disruption of the mother, it will not do to be persistent. *Image.* Dealing with the disruption of the mother means finding a way of balance.

3 *yang.* Dealing with the disruption of the father, there is a little regret but no great blame. *Image.* Deal with the disruption of the father, and in the end there is no problem.

4 *yin.* Admitting the disruption of the father, if you go you will experience shame. *Image.* Admitting the disruption of the father, you cannot go yet.

5 *yin.* Dealing with the disruption of the father, use praise. *Image.* Using praise in dealing with the father means taking up after what is virtuous and praiseworthy.

6 *yang.* Not working for kings and lords, elevate your concerns. *Image.* If it is not in the service of kings and lords, your will is exemplary.

19. OVERSEEING

For overseeing to be very successful, it is beneficial to be upright
and true. Coming to the eighth month, there
is bad luck.

OVERALL JUDGMENT

In overseeing, strength gradually increases.
Joyfully harmonizing, strength is balanced
and responsive. To achieve great success by
being upright and true is the way of heaven.
Coming to the eighth month there is bad
luck, in the sense that waning does not take
long.

IMAGE

There is earth above a marsh, symbolizing
overseeing. With inexhaustible education
and thought, the cultured embrace and pro-
tect the people without bound.

COMPONENTS

1 *yang*. Sensitive overseeing bodes well if
steadfast and true. *Image*. Sensitive overseeing bodes well if steadfast and true,

meaning that aims and actions are correct.

2 *yang.* Sensitive overseeing that bodes well would not fail to benefit anyone. *Image.* Sensitive overseeing that bodes well would not fail to benefit anyone, particularly those who are still not following directions.

3 *yin.* Childish overseeing brings in no profit. Once you get concerned about it, there will be no problem. *Image.* Childish overseeing means you are in a position you cannot manage. Once you get concerned about this, your problems will not grow.

4 *yin.* Perfect overseeing is blameless. *Image.* Perfect overseeing is blameless; your position is being properly managed.

5 *yin.* Knowledgeable overseeing is appropriate for a great leader, and it is auspicious. *Image.* What is appropriate for a great leader is balance in action.

6 *yin.* Attentive overseeing bodes well; no problem. *Image.* Attentive overseeing is auspicious insofar as the will is focused inwardly.

20. OBSERVING

Observing the ablution before the presentation of the offering, there is sincerity that is reverential.

OVERALL JUDGMENT

The great are observed on high, harmonious and gentle, showing the world balance and uprightness. Observing the ablution before the presentation of the offering, there is sincerity that is reverent; those below observe and are influenced thereby. Showing the spiritual way of Nature, the four seasons do not vary. When sages use the spiritual way to set up education the whole world follows.

IMAGE

Wind traveling over the earth symbolizes observation. Ancient kings examined the regions and observed the people to set up education.

COMPONENTS

1 *yin.* Naive observation is not blamed in ordinary people, but it is a disgrace for cul-

tured people. *Image.* Naive observation that is weak at the start is the way of ordinary people.

2 *yin.* Observing by peeking, it is advantageous to be chaste as a woman. *Image.* Observing by peeking can be embarrassing even if you are chaste as a woman.

3 *yin.* Observe the ups and downs of your own life. *Image.* Observe the ups and downs of your own life, and you have not yet lost the Way.

4 *yin.* Observing the glory of a nation, it is worthwhile being a guest of its king. *Image.* Observing the glory of nations refers to the way they value guests.

5 *yang.* Observing their own lives, cultured people are blameless. *Image.* To observe their own lives is to observe the people at large.

6 *yang.* Observing their lives, cultured people are blameless. *Image.* They observe their lives because they do not yet have peace of mind.

21. BITING THROUGH

Biting through successfully is useful in exercising justice.

OVERALL JUDGMENT

Having something in the jaws is called biting through, biting and getting through. Hardness and softness are divided, there is action and understanding. Thunder and lightning combine into a pattern. Flexibility is balanced and moving upward; even though it is not in charge, it is useful in exercising justice.

IMAGE

Thunder and lightning symbolize biting through. Ancient kings promulgated laws with clear penalties.

COMPONENTS

1 *yang.* With restraints stopping you in your tracks, you are blameless. *Image.* Restraints stopping you in your tracks means you do not act.

2 *yin.* Biting the skin, taking off the nose, you

are blameless. *Image.* Biting the skin taking off the nose stands for riding on firm strength.

3 *yin.* Biting dried meat, coming to poison, there is a little embarrassment but no blame. *Image.* Coming to poison means being out of place.

4 *yang.* Biting dried bony meat, you find a gold arrow. It is beneficial to be diligent; it bodes well to be steadfast and upright. *Image.* It is beneficial to be diligent, and it bodes well to be steadfast and upright, when you have not yet attained distinction.

5 *yin.* Biting dried meat, you find yellow gold. If you are steadfast in danger, there will be no trouble. *Image.* Being steadfast in danger, having no trouble, means finding what is right.

6 *yang.* Wearing a cangue destroying the ears is bad luck. *Image.* Wearing a cangue destroying the ears means not hearing clearly.

22. ADORNMENT

Adornment succeeds. It is beneficial to have somewhere to go on a
small scale.

OVERALL JUDGMENT

The success of adornment means flexibility
comes forth to embellish firmness; so it succeeds. Partial firmness rises to embellish
flexibility; so it is beneficial to have somewhere to go on a small scale. This is the
celestial adornment. Stabilization by civilization is the adornment of humanity. Observe
the celestial adornment to see the changes of
the seasons; observe the adornment of humanity to develop the world.

IMAGE

There is fire below a mountain, adorning it;
thus do cultured people bring clarity to government affairs without presumptuous adju-
dication.

COMPONENTS

1 *yang.* Adorning the feet, leave the car and

walk. *Image.* Leave the car and walk, when it is right not to ride.

2 *yin.* Adornment means seeking. *Image.* Adornment means seeking, rising with those above.

3 *yang.* Adorned and luxuriant, you will be lucky if you are always steadfast and true. *Image.* The luck of being forever steadfast and true is that ultimately no one demeans you.

4 *yin.* To be adorned yet plain, a white horse is swift. If there is no opposition, there is partnership. *Image.* The fourth yin is uncertain in its place. There is partnership if there is no opposition, in the sense of there being no grudge in the end.

5 *yin.* For adornment in the hills and gardens, a bolt of silk is too small. It is embarrassing, but the end is lucky. *Image.* The good luck of the fifth yin is to have joy.

6 *yang.* Plain adornment is impeccable. *Image.* Plain adornment is impeccable, for it means higher attainment of an aim.

23. STRIPPING AWAY

When stripping away, it is not advantageous to go anywhere.

OVERALL JUDGMENT

Stripping away means removal; weakness displaces strength. It is not advantageous to go anywhere; petty people are on the increase. To adapt to this to stop it, observe the images. Cultured people value the processes of waxing and waning, filling and emptying, for these are the course of Nature.

IMAGE

A mountain cleaving to earth symbolizes stripping away. Those above secure their homes by kindness to those below.

COMPONENTS

1 *yin.* Like stripping a bed of its legs, making naught of truthfulness is unlucky. *Image.* Stripping a bed of its legs means destroying a basis.

2 *yin.* Like stripping a bed of its frame, making naught of truthfulness is unlucky. *Image.*

To have stripped a bed of its frame means you have nothing to work with.

3 *yin*. Strip away so there is no blame. *Image.* Stripping away to the point where there is no blame means removing the distinction between above and below, or ruler and ruled.

4 *yin*. Stripping a bed to the skin is unlucky. *Image.* Stripping a bed to the skin means getting very close to disaster.

5 *yin*. Leading a string of fish with the favor shown to court ladies is advantageous to all. *Image.* Because of using the favor shown to court ladies, there is ultimately no resentment.

6 *yang*. A hard fruit is not consumed. Cultured people are rewarded with means of transport, petty people are stripped of their abodes. *Image.* Cultured people are rewarded with means of transport, being supported by the populace at large; petty people are stripped of their abodes, turning out to be unsuitable for employment.

24. RETURN

When return is accomplished successfully, there is exit and entry without trouble, no problem when a companion comes. Returning back over the Way, you come back in seven days. It is beneficial to have somewhere to go.

OVERALL JUDGMENT

When return is accomplished successfully is when firm strength returns to actions and operates harmoniously; this is how to go out and in without trouble, the companion whose coming means there will be no problem. Returning back over the Way, coming back in seven days, refers to the operation of Nature. It is beneficial to have somewhere to go, in that strength is growing. Return may be referred to as seeing the center of the universe.

IMAGE

Thunder inside earth symbolizes return. Thus did ancient kings shut the gates on the winter solstice; caravans did not travel, and the ruler did not inspect the provinces.

COMPONENTS

1 *yang.* If you return before going far, you will have no regret and be very lucky. *Image.* Returning before going far is done by self-cultivation.

2 *yin.* Return to goodness bodes well. *Image.* The fortune of return to goodness comes about through kindness to those below.

3 *yin.* The diligence of repeated return is blameless. *Image.* The diligence of repeated return is blameless in terms of being dutiful.

4 *yin.* With balanced action, return independently. *Image.* Returning independently with balanced action is done by following the Way.

5 *yin.* Return attentively, and you will have no regret. *Image.* Attentive return so that you have no regret means being balanced by self-examination.

6 *yin.* Return to confusion is unlucky; there will be disastrous trouble. If it motivates a

military expedition, it will wind up with a tremendous defeat, boding ill for the leader of the nation. Even in ten years there will be no victory. *Image.* What bodes ill about return to confusion is that it goes against directed guidance.

25. FIDELITY

Fidelity is very successful, beneficial if correct. If you deny what is right, you are mistaken and will not benefit from going anywhere.

OVERALL JUDGMENT

In fidelity, strength comes from outside and becomes the guiding focus within. Being active and robust, firm strength balanced and responsive, succeeding greatly in the right way is the order of Nature. If you deny what is right, you are mistaken and will not benefit from going anywhere. Where does fidelity lead? Without the help of the order of Nature, would you go?

IMAGE

Thunder travels under the sky, things go along with fidelity. Ancient kings promoted flourishing according to the seasons to nurture all beings.

COMPONENTS

1 *yang.* Proceeding without deviation bodes well. *Image.* Proceeding without deviation means attaining one's aim.

2 *yin.* If you have not plowed for the harvest and have not prepared new fields, then it is profitable to have somewhere to go. *Image.* Not having plowed for the harvest means not being rich yet.

3 *yin.* The misfortune of fidelity is like a cow someone tied being taken by a traveler, a misfortune for the townspeople. *Image.* When a passerby takes the cow, it is unfortunate for the townspeople.

4 *yang.* You should be true; then you will be blameless. *Image.* One should be true, thus being blameless; this is inherent.

5 *yang.* For the affliction of fidelity, do not

treat it with medicine; there will be joy. *Image.* If there is nothing wrong, medicine is not to be tried.

6 *yang.* If undeviating action is mistaken, there is no benefit gained. *Image.* This is the misfortune of undeviating action being thwarted at an impasse.

26. GREAT BUILDUP

Great buildup benefits the upright and true. Not eating at home is lucky. It is worthwhile crossing great rivers.

OVERALL JUDGMENT

In great buildup there is firm strength and earnest genuineness, with shining light daily renewed. Its virtues place strength on top, with esteem for the wise. To be powerful yet controlled is great rectitude. Not eating at home is lucky in the sense of nurturing the wise. It is worthwhile crossing great rivers, in response to Nature.

IMAGE

The sky in the mountains symbolizes great

buildup. Thus do cultured people record many words and deeds of the past to build up their virtue.

COMPONENTS

1 *yang.* When there is danger, it is beneficial to stop. *Image.* When there is danger it is beneficial to stop, in the sense of not getting into trouble.

2 *yang.* A car has its axles removed. *Image.* A car having its axles removed means there is no mistake within.

3 *yang.* A good horse gives chase. It is beneficial to struggle; it bodes well to be upright and true. Practicing charioteering and defense daily, it is worthwhile if there is somewhere to go. *Image.* It is worthwhile if there is somewhere to go, in the sense of conforming to a higher purpose.

4 *yin.* The horn guard of a young ox is very auspicious. *Image.* In this position it is very auspicious when there is joy.

5 *yin.* The tusks of a gelded boar are auspi-

cious. *Image.* In this position it is very auspicious when there is celebration.

6 *yang.* Coming to the crossroads of heaven, you get through successfully. *Image.* Coming to the crossroads of heaven means the Way is carried out on a large scale.

27. NOURISHMENT

Nourishment of truthfulness bodes well. Watch nourishment, and seek personal fulfillment yourself.

OVERALL JUDGMENT

Nourishment of truthfulness bodes well; you will have good luck if you develop what is right and true. Watching nourishment is watching what you foster; seeking personal fulfillment yourself is watching your own self-development. The universe fosters all beings; sages foster the wise and good, for their influence on the people in general. The timing of nourishment is very important!

IMAGE

Under a mountain is thunder, symbolizing nourishment. Cultured people deliberately guard their speech and moderate their consumption.

COMPONENTS

1 *yang.* It is bad luck to ignore your sacred tortoise and watch me with your jaw dropping. *Image.* Watching me with your jaw dropping is not worthwhile in any case.

2 *yin.* Reversed nourishment is abnormal, taking nourishment from higher ground; it is unlucky to go on an expedition. *Image.* In this position an expedition is unlucky because to go would mean loss of kindred.

3 *yin.* If you brush off nourishment, it is unlucky to persist. Do not do this for ten years; there is nothing to be gained by it. *Image.* The warning not to act this way for ten years means that the course of action is very much deranged.

4 *yin.* Reverse nourishment is lucky. A tiger watching intently, about to give chase, is not blamed. *Image.* The luck of reverse nourishment is the disbursing of blessings from above.

5 *yin*. In abnormal situations, you will be lucky if you remain steadfast and true; it is not appropriate to cross great rivers. *Image.* The luck of remaining steadfast and true is following higher ideals in a harmonious way. 6 *yang*. To be a source of nourishment is dangerous yet auspicious. *Image.* To be a source of nourishment is dangerous yet auspicious, because there is great celebration.

28. PREDOMINANCE OF THE GREAT

When the great predominates and the ridgepole bends, it is beneficial to go somewhere to be successful.

OVERALL JUDGMENT

Predominance of the great is when the great or mighty predominate. The ridgepole bending symbolizes weakness at the basis and in the outgrowths. Strength predominates, but it is centered; if it is gentle and acts pleasantly, then it will be profitable to go somewhere, for you will be successful. The timing of the great predominating is very important!

IMAGE

Moisture destroying wood symbolizes predominance of the great. As cultured people can stand alone without fear, they can withdraw from society without anxiety.

COMPONENTS

1 yin. Using plain reeds for a ceremonial placemat is blameless. *Image.* Using plain reeds for a ceremonial placemat means being flexible in a low position.

2 yang. When a withered willow produces sprouts and an old man gets a young wife, none fail to benefit. *Image.* An old man and a young wife are exceptionally companionable.

3 yang. It is bad luck when the ridgepole bends. *Image.* The bad luck of the ridgepole bending means the kind where it is impossible to help out.

4 yang. It is lucky when the ridgepole is raised, but there could be another embar-

rassment. *Image.* The luck of the ridgepole being raised is in not bending down.

5 yang. When a withered willow bears flowers and an old woman gets a young husband, there is no blame and no praise. *Image.* A withered willow may blossom, but how long can that last? For an old woman, a young husband can also be embarrassing.

6 yin. It is unlucky to get too involved and lose your head, but there is no blame. *Image.* Bad luck from getting too involved is not blameworthy.

29. CONSTANT PITFALLS

When there are constant pitfalls, if it has sincerity the thinking mind gets through successfully, and the activity has value.

OVERALL JUDGMENT

Constant pitfalls means a series of dangerous straits. As water flows without filling, go through dangerous straights without losing your faith. The thinking mind gets through successfully by using firmness in balance. Activity has value, in the sense that something worthwhile is accomplished by the undertaking.

The danger of the sky is that we cannot climb up into it; the danger of earth is the mountains, rivers, and hills. Rulers set up dangers to guard their countries. The timely use of danger is very important!

IMAGE

Water coming repeatedly symbolizes constant pitfalls. Cultured people learn to teach by constant application of virtue.

COMPONENTS

1 yin. When there are constant pitfalls, it is unlucky to go into a hole in a pit. *Image.* Going into a pit when there are constant pitfalls is the bad luck of losing the Way.

2 yang. Though there is danger in a pitfall, seek and you gain a little. *Image.* Seek and you gain a little, insofar as you have not gone beyond the mean.

3 yin. Coming and going, pitfall after pitfall,

blocked in dangerous straits, one goes into a hole in a pit. Do not do this. *Image.* Coming and going, pitfall after pitfall, means winding up never having accomplished anything.

4 *yin.* A jug of wine is accompanied by a ceremonial grain vessel. Use a plain cup. Having privately made a pledge through a window, in the end there is no blame. *Image.* The jug of wine and the ceremonial grain vessel symbolize the meeting point of the firm and the flexible.

5 *yang.* The pit is not filled completely; if it is leveled, there is no problem. *Image.* The pit not being filled means not yet being great within.

6 *yin.* Bound with rope and put in a briar patch, you are helpless for three years. Bad luck. *Image.* The bad luck of losing the way through weakness at the top lasts for three years.

30. FIRE

Fire is beneficial for the success of the upright. It is good luck to raise a female ox.

OVERALL JUDGMENT

Fire is clinging: sun and moon cling to the sky, plants cling to the earth. Clinging to what is right with double illumination develops the world. Flexibility gets through successfully by clinging to balance and rectitude; this is represented by it being lucky to raise a female ox.

IMAGE

Illumination doubled makes fire. Thus do great people shine on the four quarters with continued light.

COMPONENTS

1 *yang.* When the steps are awry, be heedful of this and you will be blameless. *Image.* When the steps are awry, heedfulness enables you to avoid blameworthy error.

2 *yin.* Yellow fire is very auspicious. *Image.* Yellow fire is very auspicious, because it

means attainment of a balanced course.

3 *yang.* In the fire of the setting sun, either you drum on a jug and sing, or you sigh the lament of the elderly, which is unfortunate. *Image.* How long can the fire of the setting sun last?

4 *yang.* Coming forth roughly results in burning out, dying, and being abandoned. *Image.* Coming on roughly is not allowed.

5 *yin.* There is weeping and lamenting, but good luck. *Image.* Good luck for the weak here is in cleaving to the rulership.

6 *yang.* A king needs to go out on an expedition; having good luck, he breaks down the chief. The captives are not of the same kind, so they are not blamed. *Image.* When a king needs to go out on an expedition, it is to straighten out the country.

31. SENSITIVITY

The success of sensitivity is beneficial for the true. It is lucky to wed a woman.

OVERALL JUDGMENT

Sensitivity means feeling. Flexibility is above and firmness is below; the two energies respond sensitively and thus get along with each other. Stable and happy, the man is humble to the woman; that is why this success is beneficial for the true, and it is lucky to wed a woman. All things and beings are produced through the sensitivity of heaven and earth. The sensitivity of sages moves people's minds so much that the world is harmonious and peaceful. Observe what they are sensitive to, and the conditions of all things in the universe can be seen.

IMAGE

A lake on top of a mountain symbolizes sensitivity. Cultured people accept others with openness.

COMPONENTS

1 *yin*. Sensitivity is in the big toe. *Image.* Sensitivity being in the big toe means the will is directed outside.

2 *yin*. Sensing the calf unlucky, it would be lucky to stay put. *Image.* In spite of bad luck, stay put and you will be lucky; that means following what is harmless.

3 *yang*. Sensitivity in the thighs is holding on to following; it is embarrassing to go on. *Image.* Sensitivity in the thighs also means not staying put; when one's wish is to follow others, what one holds on to is lowly.

4 *yang*. It is lucky to be true; regret disappears. Coming and going reflectively, companions follow your thoughts. *Image.* With the luck of being true, regret disappears; there is not yet any sense of harmfulness. Coming and going reflectively happens before greatness is attained.

5 *yang*. When sensitivity is in the flesh of the back, there is no regret. *Image.* Sensitivity being in the flesh of the back means the

mind is directed to final things.

6 *yin.* Sensitivity is in the jaws and tongue. *Image.* Sensitivity in the jaws and tongue means speaking with the mouth up close.

 ## 32. PERSISTENCE

When persistence is successful, there is no blame. It is beneficial to the true. It is worthwhile if there is somewhere to go.

OVERALL JUDGMENT

Persistence means going on for a long time. Firmness is above and flexibility is below: thunder and wind form a pair, meaning action in harmony; firmness and flexibility both respond persistently. When persistence is successful, there is no blame; it is beneficial to the true: this means persisting in the right way.

The way of heaven and earth persists forever and does not come to an end. It is worthwhile if there is a place to go; upon coming to an end, then there is a beginning.

As long as the sun and moon have the sky, they can shine forever; as long as the four seasons change, they can bring about development forever. When sages persist in their way, the whole world evolves to completeness. By observing what they persist in, the conditions of all beings in the universe can be seen.

IMAGE

Thunder and wind persist; thus do cultured people take their stand without changing place.

COMPONENTS

1 *yin.* Steadfastness in deep persistence is unlucky; no advantage is gained. *Image.* The bad luck of deep persistence is seeking depth at the very beginning.

2 *yang.* Regret vanishes. *Image.* Regret vanishes for the strong here, who are able to persist in centered balance.

3 *yang.* If you do not persist in virtue, you may bring on disgrace for that. Even if sincere, you will be humiliated. *Image.* If you do

not persist in virtue, you will not be admitted anywhere.

4 *yang.* There is no game in the fields. *Image.* If you persist in the wrong position, how can you catch game?

5 *yin.* Persisting in that virtue, faithfulness is good luck for a housewife, bad luck for a man. *Image.* For a housewife faithfulness is good luck; this means following one thing to the end. For a man managing duties, it is bad luck to go the housewife's way.

6 *yin.* It is unlucky when excitement persists. *Image.* When excitement persists in the leadership, there is utterly nothing accomplished.

33. WITHDRAWAL

When you get through successfully by withdrawal, if you are small it is beneficial to be steadfast and true.

OVERALL JUDGMENT

Getting through successfully by withdrawal means that you withdraw to get through successfully. Strength is in the appropriate position and is responsive, acting in harmony with the time. If you are small, it is beneficial to be steadfast and true, in the sense of growing gradually. The meaning of when to withdraw is very important!

IMAGE

Under the sky there are mountains, which find it inaccessible; thus do cultured people keep petty people at a distance, not disdainfully, but with dignity.

COMPONENTS

1 *yin.* When it is dangerous at the tail end of a withdrawal, do not purposely go anywhere. *Image.* How can the danger at the tail end of a withdrawal harm you if you do not go?

2 *yin.* If you fasten something with leather from a yellow ox, nothing can unloosen it. *Image.* Fastening with yellow ox hide means a firm will.

3 *yang.* Concerned withdrawal has problems and dangers. Taking care of helpers and concubines is auspicious. *Image.* The dangers of concerned withdrawal are trouble and ex-

haustion. Taking care of helpers and concubine is auspicious, but it is not enough for great works.

4 *yang.* Cultured people who withdraw in the right way are lucky; petty people do not. *Image.* Cultured people withdraw in the right way, petty people do not.

5 *yang.* A felicitous withdrawal is auspicious if right. *Image.* A felicitous withdrawal is auspicious if right, in the sense of being based on right intentions.

6 *yang.* When those who have grown rich withdraw, no one fails to benefit. *Image.* No one fails to benefit when those who have grown rich withdraw, because there is no suspicion.

34. THE POWER OF GREATNESS

The power of greatness benefits the true.

OVERALL JUDGMENT

The power of greatness is powerful. It is powerful because of strong action. The power of greatness benefits the true; that is, if the greatness is correct. Make greatness right, and the conditions of heaven and earth can be seen.

IMAGE

Thunder is up in the sky, representing the power of greatness. Whatever is improper, cultured people avoid doing.

COMPONENTS

1 yang. When the power is in the feet, it is unlucky to go on an expedition, though you have certainty. *Image.* When the power is in your feet, your certainty will wear out.

2 yang. It bodes well to be upright and true. *Image.* Strength in this position is auspicious because it is upright and true, in the sense of being centered and balanced.

3 yang. When petty people exercise power, cultured people deliberately disappear, steadfast and true, diligent in danger. If rams butt into fences, they will get their horns stuck. *Image.* When small people exercise power, cultured people dissemble.

4 *yang*. Remain steadfast and true, and you will be lucky and freed from regret. If fences give way, you do not get stuck. Power is in the gut of a great vehicle. *Image*. When fences give way, and so you do not get stuck, that means it is worthwhile going ahead.

5 *yin*. Losing the ram in ease, you have no regret. *Image*. When you lose the ram in ease, it means your position is not appropriate.

6 *yin*. A ram that has run into a fence cannot withdraw and cannot go ahead. No profit is gained. If you struggle with difficulties, you will be lucky. *Image*. Inability to withdraw or go ahead means you have not been careful to think things out thoroughly. If you struggle with difficulties, you will be lucky, insofar as faults and errors do not increase.

35. ADVANCE

Advancing, a secure lord uses gift horses in abundance, and holds meetings three times a day.

OVERALL JUDGMENT

Advance means progress, symbolized by light emerging over the earth, docilely cleaving to great illumination. Through flexibility there is progress and upward movement; this is why it says a secure lord uses gift horses in abundance and holds meetings three times a day.

IMAGE

Light emerges over the earth, advancing. Cultured people illumine virtue by reflecting it themselves.

COMPONENTS

1 *yin.* Advancing, under stress, it bodes well to be steadfast and true. If there is no trust, be magnanimous and let there be no blame. *Image.* Advancing under stress means independently doing what is right. Being magnanimous and not blaming refer to the time

before a mission has been accepted.

2 yin. Advancing, grieving, it bodes well to be steadfast and true. This great blessing is received from the grandmother. *Image.* This great blessing is received by being balanced and upright.

3 yin. When the group approves, regret vanishes. *Image.* Aims that are approved by a group make upward progress.

4 yang. Advancing like a squirrel is dangerous if constant. *Image.* It is dangerous to be constantly being like a squirrel; this means being out of place.

5 yin. When regret is gone and trust is gained, do not worry; it bodes well to go on, for none will not profit. *Image.* When trust is gained, do not worry, for if you proceed you will be glad you did.

6 yang. Advancing the horns is only used for conquering the heartland; it is dangerous, but if all goes well there is no wrong done. It is embarrassing to persist. *Image.* This is used for conquering the heartland; that is, when the Way has not yet spread greatly.

▤ 36. INJURY TO THE ENLIGHTENED

When there is injury to the enlightened, it is beneficial to be steadfast and true in distress.

OVERALL JUDGMENT

The enlightened go underground; this is when there is injury to the enlightened. Inwardly refined and illumined yet outwardly soft and docile, they therefore suffer great difficulties and hardships. It is beneficial to be steadfast and true in distress; this means concealing your illumination, making your intentions upright in spite of inner difficulties.

IMAGE

Light going into the ground symbolizes injury to the enlightened. In dealing with the masses, cultured people are deliberately unobtrusive, yet illumined.

COMPONENTS

1 yang. When the enlightened are injured in flight, they let their wings hang down. Cul-

tured people on a journey do not eat for three days. When there is somewhere to go, the person in charge has a say. *Image.* When cultured people are on a journey, it is right for them not to eat.

2 *yin.* When the enlightened are injured in the left leg, there is need for help; it is lucky if the horses are strong. *Image.* Luck for the weak in this position is to have practical models to follow.

3 *yang.* When the enlightened have been injured and go south hunting, even if the big bosses are caught they cannot be corrected quickly. *Image.* The aim of hunting in the south is a major takeover.

4 *yin.* Going in through the left belly, you find the heart of injury to the enlightened and seek to go out of the house. *Image.* Going in through the left belly means finding the intention in the mind.

5 *yin.* When injured because of enlightenment like a righteous scion of a corrupt house, it is beneficial to be upright and true. *Image.* The uprightness of a righteous scion of a

corrupt house is in the fact that illumination cannot be stopped.

6 *yin.* When not illumined, there is darkness. First you climb to the sky, later you go underground. *Image.* First climbing to the sky means lighting up the nations of the four quarters; later going underground means loss of normalcy.

37. PEOPLE IN THE HOME

For people in the home, it is beneficial for the women to be chaste.

OVERALL JUDGMENT

For people in the home, the right position for women is inside, while the right position for men is outside. For men and women to be right is of universal importance. People in the home have strict leaders, namely the father and the mother. When fathers play the role of fathers, sons play the role of sons, elder brothers play the role of elder brothers, younger brothers play the role of younger brother, husbands play the role of husbands, and wives play the role of wives, then the way of the family is right. Rectify the family, and the world will be settled.

IMAGE

Wind coming from fire symbolizes people in the home. Cultured people speak factually and act consistently.

COMPONENTS

1 *yang.* Guard the home you have, and regret vanishes. *Image.* Guarding the home you have means your aspiration has not changed.

2 *yin.* Not going anywhere, staying inside providing food, it is auspicious to be steadfast and true. *Image.* What is auspicious for the weak in this position is harmonious accord.

3 *yang.* When people in the home are strict, it is auspicious to be conscientious and diligent. When the women and children are frivolous, finally there is shame. *Image.* When the people in the home are strict, that means they have not slipped. When the women and children are frivolous, that means the order of the household is lost.

4 *yin.* Enriching the home is very auspicious. *Image.* Enriching the home is very auspicious; this means harmony being in place.

5 *yang.* When the king comes to have a home, do not worry. It is auspicious. *Image.* The king coming to have a home means partners loving each other.

6 *yang.* If there is truthfulness, awesomeness bodes well in the end. *Image.* What bodes well about awesomeness refers to self-examination and reform.

38. OPPOSITION

When there is opposition, it is lucky if it is a small matter.

OVERALL JUDGMENT

In opposition, fire moves upward and moisture moves downward; two women live together but their wills do not go the same way. Joyfully clinging to light, flexibility progressing upward, action attains centered balance and responds to firm strength. This is why it is lucky if it is a small affair. Sky and earth are opposite, yet their work is the same; males and females are opposite, yet their wills commune. All beings are different, but their concerns are similar. The timely use of opposition is very important!

IMAGE

Fire above and moisture below symbolize opposition. Cultured people assimilate yet are different.

COMPONENTS

1 *yang.* Regret disappears. If you lose the horse, do not chase it; it will return on its own. If you see evil people, you will be blameless. *Image.* Seeing evil people means you thereby avoid error.

2 *yang.* When you meet the master in an alley, there is no blame. *Image.* When you meet the master in an alley, that means you have not lost the Way.

3 *yin.* Having the vehicle dragged and the ox halted, that person is being punished by heaven. Though there was no beginning,

there will be a conclusion. *Image.* Having the vehicle dragged means the position is not appropriate. Though there was no beginning, there will be a conclusion; that is, on meeting the firm and strong.

4 *yang.* When isolated by opposition, if you meet good people, interact truthfully, and you will be impeccable even in danger. *Image.* Impeccability through truthful interaction means aims are carried out through purposeful action.

5 *yin.* Regret disappears. When the clan has punished its own, what is wrong with proceeding onward? *Image.* When the clan has punished its own, it will be joyful to proceed onward.

6 *yang.* When you are isolated by opposition, you see pigs covered with mire and a wagonload of demons. The bows drawn at first are the bows later put down. They are not enemies but partners. Proceeding onward, it is lucky if rain is encountered. *Image.* The luck of encountering rain means that all sorts of doubts and suspicions disappear.

39. HALTING

For halting, the southwest is advantageous, not the northeast. It is worthwhile to see great people. It bodes well to be steadfast and true.

OVERALL JUDGMENT

Halting means trouble, danger ahead. To be able to stop on seeing danger is knowledge. For halting the southeast is advantageous; this means proceeding to gain centered balance. The northeast is not advantageous; this refers to a way that winds up at an impasse. It is worthwhile seeing great people, in that something is accomplished by going to them. When in the appropriate position, it bodes well to be steadfast and true, thus to right the nation. The timely use of halting is very important!

IMAGE

Above a mountain is water; halt. Cultured people develop virtues by self-examination.

COMPONENTS

1 *yin.* When going is halted, coming is

praised. *Image.* When going is halted, coming is praised, meaning that it is best to wait for the right time.

2 *yin.* When kings and ministers halt at trouble, it is not for personal reasons. *Image.* When kings and ministers halt at trouble, ultimately there is no difference.

3 *yang.* When going is halted, come back. *Image.* When going is halted, come back; those at home will be glad.

4 *yin.* When going is halted, come with company. *Image.* When going is halted, come with company, so that the position be fulfilled.

5 *yang.* At a major halt, friends come. *Image.* At a major halt, friends come with balance and moderation.

6 *yin.* When going is halted, coming is great. It is worthwhile seeing great people. *Image.* When going is halted, coming is great; this means that the will is within. It is worthwhile seeing great people, as a means of following what is noble and worthy.

40. SOLUTION

For a solution, there is profit in the southwest. Without having gone anywhere, the coming back is auspicious. If there is somewhere to go, it bodes well to be early.

OVERALL JUDGMENT

Solution involves action because of danger, acting so as to escape from danger. For a solution there is profit in the southwest, meaning that proceeding onward wins people. Without having gone anywhere, the coming back is auspicious; this means attainment of centered balance. If there is somewhere to go, it bodes well to be early; this means there is something to be accomplished by proceeding onward. With the resolution of heaven and earth, it thunders and rains. When it thunders and rains, the sprouts of fruitful plants and trees all shed their sheaths. The time of solution is very important!

IMAGE

Thunder and rain symbolize solution. Thus do cultured people forgive mistakes and pardon wrongs.

COMPONENTS

1 yin. Be impeccable. *Image.* Where firmness and flexibility meet, it is right to be impeccable.

2 yang. Catching three foxes on a hunt, finding a golden arrow, you will be lucky if upright and true. *Image.* The strong in this position will be lucky if upright and true, in the sense of attaining the way of centered balance.

3 yin. Being dependent yet opportunistic brings on enemies; it is shameful to persist. *Image.* Being dependent yet opportunistic is indeed shameful. If you bring attack on yourself by yourself, who else is there to blame?

4 yang. When you remove your big toe, friends come to this sincerity. *Image.* Removing your big toe means realizing you are not in the appropriate position.

5 yin. It is cultured people who have a solution that bodes well. They have sincerity toward ordinary people. *Image.* When cultured people have a solution, ordinary people step back.

6 yin. A lord deliberately shoots a hawk on a high wall; getting it will benefit all. *Image.* A lord deliberately shooting a hawk means a resolution of discord.

 ## 41. REDUCTION

Reduction is very auspicious and blameless if there is truthfulness. It is appropriate to be steadfast and upright. It is worthwhile going somewhere. What is to be used? Two bowls can be used for presentation.

OVERALL JUDGMENT

Reduction means reducing the lower to augment the higher; its course proceeds upward. If there is truthfulness in reduction, it is very auspicious and blameless. It is well to be steadfast and upright, and it is profitable to have somewhere to go. What is to be used? Two bowls can be used for presentation. The two bowls must be timed appropriately: reduction of firmness and increase of flexibility have their times, as reduction and increase, filling and emptying, go along with the time.

IMAGE

There is a lake below a mountain, symbolizing reduction. Thus do cultured people eliminate wrath and stop cupidity.

COMPONENTS

1 *yang.* Concluding your business, go right away, and there is no blame; but assess before reducing this. *Image.* Concluding your business and going right away means joining higher aims.

2 *yang.* It is beneficial to be steadfast and true, but it would be unlucky to go on an expedition. Do not decrease, but increase this. *Image.* For the strong in this position, it is beneficial to be steadfast and true, and this is to be considered their aim.

3 *yin.* When three people travel, they reduce a single person. One person traveling gets suitable companionship. *Image.* When one acts as an individual, a group is suspicious.

4 *yin.* Reducing the ailment, causing prompt rejoicing, there is no problem. *Image.* If you reduce the ailment, that is indeed something to be glad about.

5 *yin.* If given ten pairs of tortoises, no one is able to oppose. Very lucky. *Image.* The great good luck of the weak in this position is help from above.

6 *yang.* Do not decrease, but increase this. There will be no blame. It bodes well to be steadfast and true. It is beneficial to have somewhere to go; you find helpers but have no house. *Image.* Do not decrease, but increase this, meaning full attainment of your aim.

42. INCREASE

Increase is worthwhile if it is going somewhere. It is worthwhile to cross great rivers.

OVERALL JUDGMENT

Increase means decreasing the higher to add to the lower; the delight of the people is boundless. Going down from the higher to the lower, that path is very brilliant. It is worthwhile if it is going somewhere, meaning that there will be happiness if you are balanced and upright. It is worthwhile to cross great rivers, meaning that the path of harmonious action is carried out. Increase is active, in a harmonious way, progressing day by day, without bound. As heaven disburses and earth produces, their increase is universal. In any case, the path of increase goes along with the time.

IMAGE

Wind and thunder symbolize increase. When cultured people see good, they take to it; and when they have made a mistake, they correct it.

COMPONENTS

1 *yang.* When it is profitable to do major works, if they are very auspicious there is no problem. *Image.* There is no problem if the works are very auspicious, meaning that subordinates are not overlooked.

2 *yin.* If given ten pairs of tortoises, no one can oppose. It is auspicious to be eternally steadfast and true. It is auspicious for the king to purposefully make offerings to God. *Image.* That something is given means it comes from outside.

3 *yin.* There is no blame in using unfortunate events for enhancement. Be sincere and balanced in conduct; when making announcements to lords, use a symbol of authority. *Image.* Use of unfortunate events for enhancement is something that has always existed.

4 *yin.* Balanced conduct expressed publicly is followed. It is an advantage when needed for

use as a basis to move a homeland. *Image.* What the public will follow when it is expressed is the will to help make beneficial improvements.

5 *yang.* To have sincerity blesses the heart, without question. Very auspicious. To have sincerity blesses one with rewards for virtue. *Image.* To have sincerity blesses the heart; do not question it. It blesses one with rewards for virtue, major attainment of aims.

6 *yang.* Do not increase something so much that it might be attacked; when you set your mind to something, do not be so persistent that it leads to bad luck. *Image.* To say that something should not be increased so much generally refers to partiality; to say that it might be attacked refers to what comes from outside.

43. DECISIVENESS

Decisiveness is brought up at the royal court. There is a sincere cry about the existence of danger. Address your own domain. It is not profitable to go right to war. It is profitable to get somewhere.

OVERALL JUDGMENT

Decisiveness means making distinctions, strength separating out weakness. It involves being powerful yet pleasant, decisive yet harmonious. When it is brought up at the royal court, this indicates a situation where weakness is riding on top of five times as much strength. If there is a sincere cry about the existence of danger, that caution sheds light. Address your own domain; you will not profit from going right to war, for this preference would lead to desperate straits. It is profitable to get somewhere, for the growth of strength will then be finished.

IMAGE

Water rising into the sky symbolizes removal. Cultured people distribute their wealth to reach those below them, but if they are proud of their virtue, they are resented.

COMPONENTS

1 *yang.* When powerful in the advancing feet, it is blameworthy to proceed unsuccessfully. *Image.* To proceed incompetently is faulty.

2 *yang.* When wary and alert, even if there are attackers in the night, there is no worry. *Image.* There is no worry even if there are attackers when you have attained a way of balance.

3 *yang.* Vigor in the face can be bad luck. Cultured people decisively travel alone; encountering rain, if they get wet there is irritation but no blame. *Image.* If cultured people are decisive, they will be blameless in the end.

4 *yang.* When there is no flesh on the buttocks, the gait is halting. Lead sheep by a rope and regret is gone. One may hear words without believing. *Image.* To say the gait is halting means the position is not appropri-

ate. To say one hears words without believing means hearing is not clear.

5 *yang.* Pleasant yet decisive, balanced behavior is blameless. *Image.* When balanced behavior is not blamed, balance is still not glorified.

6 *yin.* Without an alert, there is bad luck in the end. *Image.* The bad luck of having no alert is finally being unable to continue any longer.

44. MEETING

If a woman is strong in a meeting, do not try to marry her.

OVERALL JUDGMENT

A meeting is an encounter, the soft encountering the hard; they should not try to marry, because they cannot last together. When heaven and earth meet, things and beings appear. When firmness meets balance and rectitude, the whole world works well. The meaning of timing in meeting is very important!

IMAGE

There is wind under the sky, symbolizing meeting. Thus do leaders give out directions to announce to the four quarters.

COMPONENTS

1 *yin.* Applying a metal brake, it bodes well to be steadfast and true. If you go somewhere you will see misfortune; an emaciated pig leaps in earnest. *Image.* You apply a metal brake when drawn by weakness.

2 *yang.* When the fish is in the bag, there is no problem, but it does not benefit a guest. *Image.* Having a fish in the bag refers to an obligation that does not extend to guests.

3 *yang.* When there is no flesh on the buttocks, the gait is halting. Stir yourself to higher effort, and there will be no major problem. *Image.* That the gait is halting means that behavior is as yet inconsistent.

4 *yang.* Having no fish in the bag causes bad luck. *Image.* The bad luck of having no fish refers to estrangement of the people.

5 *yang.* Wrapping a melon with river willows

is concealing beauty. There is a descent from heaven. *Image.* For the strong in this position to conceal beauty means to be balanced and upright. Having a descent from heaven means being determined not to give up on destiny.

6 *yang.* Meeting the horns is shameful, but there is no blame. *Image.* Meeting the horns is the shame of exhaustion at the top.

45. GATHERING

Gathering leads to success; the king goes to his shrine. It is worthwhile seeing great people to attain success. It is beneficial to be true. It bodes well to make a great sacrifice. It is profitable to have somewhere to go.

OVERALL JUDGMENT

Gathering means an assembly. Harmonious and pleasant, strength is balanced and responsive; thus a gathering assembles. The king going to his shrine means making offerings of filial piety. It is worthwhile seeing great people to attain success, in the sense of gathering around what is right; so it is beneficial to be true. It bodes well to make a great sacrifice, and it is profitable to have somewhere to go; these mean following the direction of heaven. Observe the focus of their gatherings, and the conditions of all beings in the universe can be seen.

IMAGE

Moisture rises on top of the earth, gathering. Cultured people use defensive weapons to be prepared for the unexpected.

COMPONENTS

1 yin. When there is sincerity that does not last to the end, there is chaos and mobbing. When you cry, part of it is laughter. Do not worry; if you go, there will be no problem. *Image.* Chaos and mobbing mean that their minds are confused.

2 yin. Attract good luck, and there is no problem. If you are sincere, it is worthwhile to use ceremony. *Image.* There is no problem if you attract good luck, because it means there has been no change in centered balance.

3 *yin.* When gathering and lamentation go together, it profits nothing. Go, and there will be no blame, just a little embarrassment. *Image.* Go, and there will be no blame, insofar as there is accord above.

4 *yang.* Great good luck is not blamed. *Image.* When there is no blame only if there is very good luck, that means the position is not appropriate.

5 *yang.* When they are gathered around the holding of rank, no one blames the insincere. If the basis is always true, regret disappears. *Image.* To gather around the holding of rank means your aspiration is not yet great.

6 *yin.* Holdings given away, crying and snuffling, there is no blame. *Image.* Holdings given away, crying and snuffling, means not resting secure at the top.

46. RISING

Rising is a great success; thereby you will see great people, so do not worry. An expedition south bodes well.

OVERALL JUDGMENT

Flexibly adapt to the time, and you will rise. Harmonious and receptive, responding with strength in balance, this is the way to great success. Thereby you will see great people, so do not worry; that is, there will be felicity. An expedition south bodes well, meaning your purpose is carried out.

IMAGE

In the earth grow trees, rising. Thus by being careful of virtues, cultured people build up the small to lofty grandeur.

COMPONENTS

1 *yin.* Rising by truthfulness is very auspicious. *Image.* Rising by truthfulness is very auspicious; it means a higher meeting of minds.

2 *yang.* If you are sincere, then it is worthwhile using ceremony, so there is no blame.

Image. When the strong in this position are sincere, there is gladness.

3 *yang.* Rise through an empty realm. *Image.* Rising through an empty realm means there is nothing that makes you hesitate.

4 *yin.* When the king makes offerings on the mountain, if there is good luck there is no blame. *Image.* The king making offerings on the mountain means doing what you have to do.

5 *yin.* Steadfastness bodes well; ascend the steps. *Image.* Steadfastness bodes well, ascend the steps: this means fully accomplishing your purpose.

6 *yin.* Rising in the unknown benefits from unending steadfastness. *Image.* When rising in the unknown, if you fade away at the top, you will not prosper.

47. EXHAUSTION

Exhausted, yet getting through successfully, great people who are steadfast and true are lucky and blameless. There are words that are not believed.

OVERALL JUDGMENT

In exhaustion, strength is covered over. It seems only cultured people can be joyful even in straits and not lose the way to get through successfully. Great people who are steadfast and true are lucky, because their strength is balanced. There are words that are not believed, meaning that you will come to an impasse if you place a high value on talk.

IMAGE

A lake with no water symbolizes exhaustion. Cultured people achieve their purposes by living out their destiny.

COMPONENTS

1 *yin.* Seated exhausted on a tree stump, gone into a dark valley, one is not seen for three years. *Image.* Having gone into a dark

valley means there is obscurity, lack of clarity.

2 *yang.* When you are exhausted of food and drink, the regal garment then comes; it is worthwhile to purposely make ceremonial offerings. The bad luck of a military expedition is not faulted. *Image.* To be exhausted of food and drink means to have joyful celebration at heart.

3 *yin.* Exhausted on a rock, resting on brambles, going into one's chamber but not seeing one's wife is unlucky. *Image.* Resting on brambles means riding on the obdurate. Going into one's chamber but not seeing one's wife is ominous.

4 *yang.* Slow to arrive, exhausted in a gold car, it is embarrassing, but there is a conclusion. *Image.* Being slow to arrive means the aspiration is on something lower. Although one is out of place, there is partnership.

5 *yang.* Nose and feet cut off, exhausted in a regal robe. After that there gradually comes to be joy. It is worthwhile making ceremonial offerings. *Image.* Having the nose and

feet cut off means that aspirations have not been attained. After that there gradually comes to be joy; that is, if you are balanced and straightforward. It is worthwhile making ceremonial offerings, for the blessings received.

6 *yin.* Exhausted in entanglements in insecure situations, there will be regret if one thinks action will bring regret. It bodes well to go forth. *Image.* To be exhausted in entanglements is to have not yet mastered what is before you. That there will be regret if action is regretted means that good luck is operative.

48. THE WELL

When there is a well, changing a town does not change the well. There is neither loss nor gain. There are goings and comings, but the well remains a well. One that almost reaches is still not rope enough for hauling from the well. Breaking the bucket is bad luck.

OVERALL JUDGMENT

Wind under water, making the water rise, symbolizes a well. A well nourishes without being exhausted. Changing the town does not change the well; this means acting with firm strength and centered balance. Losing nothing and gaining nothing, whatever the comings and goings, the well is a well. If it almost reaches, it is still not a sufficient rope for hauling water from the well; this refers to when one has not yet accomplished anything successfully. Breaking the bucket refers to the way bad luck happens.

IMAGE

There is water over wood, symbolizing a well. Cultured people encourage reciprocity by comforting the common folk.

COMPONENTS

1 *yin.* Mud in a well is not drunk. At an abandoned well there are no beasts. *Image.* Mud in the well is not drunk, being at the bottom. That there are no beasts at an abandoned well means being left behind by the times.

2 *yang.* The depths of the well provide enough for a minnow; the jar is broken and leaks. *Image.* The depths of the well providing only enough for a minnow represents having no associates.

3 *yang.* When a well is cleared but not partaken of, it is a pain to one's heart. It can be drawn upon, and when the ruler understands, all will receive its blessings. *Image.* When a well is cleared but not partaken of, that means practical steps are a painful worry. Seeking the understanding of the ruler is to receive blessings.

4 *yin.* When a well is tiled there is no problem. *Image.* When a well is tiled there is no problem; this means repairing the well.

5 *yang.* When a well is pure, its cold spring is partaken of. *Image.* Partaking of a cold spring means being balanced and upright.

6 *yin.* While the well is being drawn from, do not cover it. Truthfulness is very auspicious. *Image.* Great luck is major achievement at the top.

49. CHANGE

Change proves true on the day it is finished. For great success, it is profitable to be upright and true; then regret disappears.

OVERALL JUDGMENT

Change is symbolized by water and fire extinguishing and evaporating each other. Two women living together but at cross-purposes represent change. It proves true on the day it is finished; when the change has happened, then it is believed. When it is civilized and pleasing, very successful because it is right, and the change is appropriate, the regret then disappears. As heaven and earth change, the four seasons take place. When ancient rulers changed the social order, they followed Nature and responded to humanity. The timing of change is very important!

IMAGE

There is fire in a lake, symbolizing change. Cultured people define the seasons clearly by making calendars.

COMPONENTS

1 *yang.* Use the hide of a yellow ox for firm stability. *Image.* Use the hide of a yellow ox for firm stability; that is, when it is inappropriate to act on anything.

2 *yin.* On the day it is done, then you have changed something. It bodes well to proceed; there will be no problem. *Image.* On the day it is done, the execution of change is praiseworthy.

3 *yang.* When an expedition bodes ill, it is dangerous to persist. When talk of change is successful three times, there is truth to it. *Image.* When talk of change works out three times, then where to go?

4 *yang.* When regret disappears and it is trustworthy, a revolution bodes well. *Image.* What bodes well for a revolution is trust in its purpose.

5 *yang.* Great people change like tigers. They have certainty without arguing. *Image.* That great people change like tigers means that their patterns are clearly evident.

6 *yin.* Cultured people change like leopards;

ordinary people change their outward appearances. When it bodes ill to go on an expedition, it bodes well to abide steadfastly. *Image.* That cultured people change like leopards means their patterns are intricate. That ordinary people change their outward appearances means they conform to the leaders they follow.

50. THE CAULDRON

The cauldron symbolizes great fortune and success.

OVERALL JUDGMENT

The cauldron is a symbol, using wood, wind, and fire to successfully cook to perfection. Sages cook to make offerings to God, and their great offering is made by nurturing the wise. Penetrating, brilliantly clear of eye and ear, making upward progress, balanced in action and cooperating with the strong: this is the way to great success.

IMAGE

There is fire over wood, symbolizing a cauldron. Cultured people stabilize their lives in the right position.

COMPONENTS

1 *yin.* When a cauldron is overturned on its base, that facilitates removal of anything bad. When one takes a concubine, as long a she has a son there is no blame. *Image.* When a cauldron is overturned on its base, that is not necessarily bad; it facilitates removal of anything bad, in favor of something worthwhile.

2 *yang.* When there is substance in the cauldron, if my antagonists harbor jealousy, it is lucky if it cannot affect me. *Image.* The presence of substance in the cauldron means prudence about where one goes. If my antagonist harbors jealousy, we will never be on intimate terms.

3 *yang.* When the knobs of the cauldron are changed, the function is inhibited; pheasant fat is not eaten. Just when it rains, that decreases regret, and there is good fortune in the end. *Image.* The knobs of a cauldron being changed means failure at one's duty.

4 *yang.* When the cauldron breaks its legs, spilling the ducal repast, the punishment is severe; bad luck. *Image.* Spilling the ducal repast means trustworthiness is questionable.

5 *yin.* When a cauldron has gold knobs and a jade handle, it profits the upright and true. *Image.* Gold knobs on a cauldron represent using centered balance for fulfillment.

6 *yang.* A jade handle on a cauldron is very auspicious, beneficial all around. *Image.* The jade handle is on the top; this means the junction of firmness and flexibility.

 51. THUNDER

Thunder means getting through successfully: when thunder comes there is alarm, then the mirth of laughing talk. Thunder startling for a hundred miles does not cause loss of serious devotion.

OVERALL JUDGMENT

Thunder means getting through successfully: when thunder comes there is alarm, meaning that fear brings on good fortune; then the mirth of laughing talk, meaning that af-

terward there is a model. Thunder startles
for a hundred miles; it startles those far away
and frightens those nearby. By serious devotion it is possible to safeguard the heritage
and the land, thus acting in a role of sacred
leadership.

IMAGE

Repeated thunder causes a stir. Cultured
people practice self-examination with trepi-
dation and fear.

COMPONENTS

1 *yang*. When thunder comes there is fearful
alarm; it is auspicious if there is the sound of
mirthful talk afterward. *Image.* When thunder comes there is fearful alarm; fear may
bring fortune. The mirthful talk means that
there is an example afterward.

2 *yin*. Thunder coming is dangerous. Re-
membering the loss of a treasure, you climb
up nine hills, but should not pursue, for you
will get it in seven days. *Image.* The danger
of thunder coming is riding on the unyield-
ing.

3 *yin.* When thunder is faint, stir into action and there will be no fault. *Image.* Thunder being faint means being in a position that is not appropriate.

4 *yang.* Thunder falls in the mud. *Image.* Thunder falling in the mud means not having achieved greatness.

5 *yin.* Thunder coming and going is dangerous. Remember there is no loss, and there is something to do. *Image.* The danger of thunder coming and going means acting in peril. The thing to do is to remain balanced in the center; then there is indeed no loss.

6 *yin.* Thunder trailing off, the gaze unsteady, an expedition bodes ill. When thunder does not affect the individual, but does affect the neighborhood, there is no blame. If a partnership is formed, there is talk. *Image.* Thunder trailing off means centered balance has not been attained. In spite of foreboding, there is no blame, because of being awed by the lesson of the neighbors.

52. MOUNTAINS

Mountains stand back to back. If you do not recognize yourself, and while going through the yard do not see the people, there is no blame.

OVERALL JUDGMENT

Mountains represent stopping. When it is time to be still, then stop; when it is time to act, then go ahead. When action and stillness do not miss their timing, the path is illumined. Mountains mean stillness, in the sense of stopping or staying in the appropriate place. When those above and those below are opposed to each other, they do not have anything to do with each other. This is why there is no blame when you do not recognize yourself and do not see the people while going through the yard.

IMAGE

As the mountains are stationary, cultured people think without getting out of place.

COMPONENTS

1 *yin.* Stop the feet, and there is no problem. It is beneficial to be ever steadfast and true. *Image.* Stopping the feet means stopping before you have taken a misstep.

2 *yin.* If stopping the calves does not save them from following, the heart is unhappy. *Image.* Not saving them from following means not having withdrawn obediently.

3 *yang.* Stopping at the boundary breaks continuity; danger influences the heart. *Image.* Because you are stopping at the limit, the danger influences your heart.

4 *yin.* Stop the body, and there is no fault. *Image.* Stopping the body means putting a halt to things in your own person.

5 *yin.* Still the jaws, be orderly in speech, and regret disappears. *Image.* Stabilize the jaws with balance and accuracy.

6 *yang.* Careful stopping is auspicious. *Image.* The good fortune of careful stopping is having gone through to the end with attentive care.

53. GRADUAL PROGRESS

Gradual progress is auspicious for the marriage of a woman; it is helpful to be chaste.

OVERALL JUDGMENT

Gradual progress bodes well for the marriage of a woman. When progress is made to the proper stage, the procedure is successful. By progressing in the right way, it is possible to straighten out the country. The proper stage is when strength is in balance. When calm and harmonious, action does not come to an impasse.

IMAGE

There are trees on a mountain, growing gradually. Cultured people improve mores by living with wisdom and virtue.

COMPONENTS

1 *yin.* As geese gradually make their way onto shore, if the little ones struggle, there is advice, not blame. *Image.* It is right that the struggle of little ones not be blamed.

2 *yin.* It is auspicious if geese gradually make

their way onto a boulder and eat and drink happily. *Image.* Eating and drinking happily is not idly stuffing yourself.

3 *yang.* Geese gradually making their way to high ground, it is inauspicious if the husband goes off on an expedition and does not return, and the wife conceives but does not nurture. It is useful to deliberately ward off enmity. *Image.* The husband going off on an expedition and not returning represents the disgrace of leaving the group. The wife conceiving but not nurturing represents deviation from the right way. It is useful to deliberately ward off enmity, meaning to get along for mutual security.

4 *yin.* When geese gradually go up in a tree, if they find a level roost they will have no trouble. *Image.* If they find a level roost means if they get in by conformity.

5 *yang.* As a goose gradually proceeding onto a hill, a wife does not conceive for three years; ultimately no one can overcome her. This is auspicious. *Image.* What is auspicious

about being invincible to the end is attaining what one wishes.

6 *yang.* When geese gradually proceed onto high ground, their feathers can be used for ceremonies; this is auspicious. *Image.* It is auspicious when the feathers can be used for ceremonies; this means one is not susceptible to confusion.

54. A YOUNG WOMAN GOING TO MARRY

For a young woman going to marry, an expedition bodes ill, with nothing gained.

OVERALL JUDGMENT

Marriage is an important matter for heaven and earth. If heaven and earth do not commune, nothing flourishes. Marriage is an end and a beginning for people. When she acts because of attraction, the one who is married is an immature girl. An expedition bodes ill because it is out of place; nothing is gained, for the weak rides on the strong.

IMAGE

There is thunder over a lake, symbolizing a young woman going to marry. Cultured people know what is wrong by reflecting on lasting results.

COMPONENTS

1 *yang*. When a young woman going to marry becomes a junior wife, the lame can walk, and it bodes well to go on. *Image.* When a young woman going to marry becomes a junior wife, that means she is constant; the good fortune of the lame walking means mutual assistance.

2 *yang*. When only vaguely able to see, it is beneficial to be as steadfast and true as a recluse. *Image.* It is beneficial to be as steadfast and true as a recluse, in the sense of unvarying constancy.

3 *yin*. When a young woman going to marry does so with expectations, instead she marries as a junior wife. *Image.* For a young woman going to marry to do so with expectations means being in a position that is not yet appropriate.

4 *yang.* When a young woman going to marry postpones the date, she delays marrying until the right time. *Image.* The purpose of postponing a date is to act only under certain conditions.

5 *yin.* When the emperor marries off his younger sister, the attire of the princess is not as good as that of the ladies in waiting. The moon almost full, the outlook is good. *Image.* When the emperor marries off his younger sister, she is not garbed as nicely as the ladies in waiting; that means being poised in balance and behaving with nobility.

6 *yin.* When the woman receives a chest with no content, and the man sacrifices a goat but there is no blood, nothing is gained. *Image.* Weakness at the top is insubstantiality, like coming into possession of an empty coffer.

55. ABUNDANCE

Abundance is success; kings aggrandize it. Do not worry; it is good for the sun to be at midpoint.

OVERALL JUDGMENT

Abundance means magnitude. Understanding applied in action results in abundance. Kings aggrandizing it means valuing magnitude. Do not worry, for it is good when the sun is at midpoint: this means it is good to light up the whole world. When the sun has reached midpoint, then it starts to decline; when the moon has waxed full, then it begins to wane. Even heaven and earth fill up and empty out, waxing and waning with the seasons; how much more so with humans, or with ghosts and spirits!

IMAGE

Thunder and lightning both come, representing abundance. Cultured people make judgments and pass sentences.

COMPONENTS

1 *yang.* Meeting the leading partner, even as

equals there is no blame. It will be valuable to go on. *Image.* That there is no blame even as equals means it is disastrous to go past equality.

2 *yin.* When abundance is a shade, you see the north star in the daytime. To go on will get you suspicion and disdain. It is auspicious if you are truthful in an evident way. *Image.* To be truthful in an evident way means to express your aims and purposes frankly.

3 *yang.* When abundance is a downpour, you see droplets in the sun. Breaking your right arm, there is no blame. *Image.* When there is an abundant downpour means when it is not feasible to do great works. Breaking your right arm means turning out unusable.

4 *yang.* When abundance is a shade, you see the north star in the daytime. It is auspicious if you meet the hidden master. *Image.* When abundance is a shade is when one's position is not appropriate. Seeing the north star in daytime refers to obscurity and lack of clarity. Meeting the hidden master is an auspicious undertaking.

5 yin. It is auspicious when bringing about excellence results in celebration and praise. *Image.* For the weak in this position it is lucky to have something to celebrate.

6 yin. When you make your rooms huge and enclose your house, a peek in the door finds it silent, with no one there, not to be seen for three years. *Image.* Huge rooms mean soaring to the edge of the sky with pride. A peek in the door finding it silent, with no one there, means keeping to oneself.

56. TRAVEL

Travel is successful when minimal; when traveling it bodes well to be steadfast.

OVERALL JUDGMENT

Travel is successful when minimal. Flexibility is balanced outwardly and harmonizes with firm strength, remaining calm and cleaving to understanding. This is why it is successful when minimal, and it bodes well to be steadfast when traveling. The meaning of the timing of travel is very important!

IMAGE

There is fire on top of a mountain symbolizing travel. Cultured people apply punishment prudently with understanding, and do not keep people imprisoned.

COMPONENTS

1 yin. In traveling, exhaustion is the trouble it brings on. *Image.* Exhaustion on a journey is the calamity of frustration.

2 yin. Coming to an inn on your travels, keep your money with you and you will gain the loyalty of servants. *Image.* Gaining the loyalty of servants means there is ultimately no resentment.

3 yang. When traveling, if you burn the inn and lose your servants, you are in danger even if steadfast. *Image.* If you burn the inn when traveling, you too will be injured thereby. if you travel with subordinates in this way, it is right that you lose them.

4 yang. Staying somewhere on a journey, one may get resources and tools, but the heart is not happy. *Image.* Staying somewhere on a

journey means one has not obtained a position; then even if one gets resources and tools, one's heart is not yet happy.

5 *yin*. Shooting a pheasant, one arrow is lost. In the end one is appointed with honor. *Image*. To finally be appointed with honor means to attain higher goals.

6 *yang*. A bird burning its nest, the traveler first laughs and then later cries. Losing an ox at ease is unlucky. *Image*. When travel is at the peak, it is right to burn the nest; the misfortune of losing an ox while at ease is never even noticing.

57. CONFORMITY

Conforming, the small succeed; it is beneficial to have somewhere to go, and it is beneficial to see great people.

OVERALL JUDGMENT

Double conformity is used to express repetition of directions. Strength conforms to balance and correctness, so what is willed is carried out in action. The weak all go along with the strong, so this is why the small suc-

ceed, profiting by having somewhere to go,
and profiting from seeing great people.

IMAGE

Following wind represents conformity. Cultured people repeat directions to get things
done.

COMPONENTS

1 *yin.* When going forward and backward, it
is helpful to be as steadfast as a soldier. *Image.* Going forward and backward means
one's purpose is wavering. It is helpful to be
as steadfast as a soldier, meaning that one's
purpose is settled.

2 *yang.* When conformity is more lowly than
normal, it bodes well to use intermediaries a
lot, so there will be no blame. *Image.* A lot
bodes well, that is, provided you attain balance.

3 *yang.* Repetitious conformity is embarrassing. *Image.* The embarrassment of repetitious
conformity is frustration.

4 *yin.* When regret disappears, you catch
three kinds of game on a hunt. *Image.* Catching three kinds of game on a hunt means

something is successfully accomplished.

5 yang. It bodes well to be steadfast and true; regret vanishes, and it is advantageous all around. Though there is no beginning, there is a conclusion. It bodes well to be careful before a change and reflective after a change. *Image.* What bodes well for the strong in this position is to be correctly balanced.

6 yang. When conformity is more lowly than normal, you lose your resources and tools, so it is unlucky even if you are steadfast. *Image.* If conformity is more lowly than normal, one is helpless in a position of leadership; the loss of one's resources and tools is indeed bad luck.

58. PLEASING

For pleasing to succeed, it helps to be correct.

OVERALL JUDGMENT

Pleasing means delighting. Strength balanced, flexible outside, pleasing thus benefits the upright. This is the way to accord with

Nature and respond to humanity: when the
people are led in a pleasing way, the people
forget their toil; when difficulties are faced
in a pleasing way, the people are mindless of
dying. The importance of pleasing is how the
people are encouraged.

IMAGE

Joined lakes symbolize pleasing. Cultured
people form associations for learning.

COMPONENTS

1 *yang*. Pleasing by harmonizing bodes well.
Image. What bodes well about pleasing by
harmonizing is that actions are not doubted.

2 *yang*. Pleasing by sincerity bodes well; regret disappears. *Image.* What bodes well
about pleasing by sincerity is trusting intentions.

3 *yin*. Forced pleasing bodes ill. *Image.* What
bodes ill about forced pleasing is being out
of place.

4 *yang*. Calculated pleasing is uneasy; firmly
disdain it, and there will be rejoicing. *Image.*
Joy for the strong in this position is having
something to celebrate.

5 yang. There is danger in trusting usurpers.
Image. For trusting usurpers, the position is
just right.
6 yin. Attraction pleases. *Image.* For the weak
in this position, pleasing by attraction is not
yet glorious.

59. DISPERSAL

Dispersal successful, a king comes
to have a shrine. It is worthwhile
crossing great rivers, beneficial if correct.

OVERALL JUDGMENT

Dispersal is successful: strength comes inex-
haustibly, flexibility finds its place outwardly, and there is assimilation upward.
The king coming to have a shrine means that
the ruler is now in the center. It is worthwhile crossing great rivers, in the sense that
something is accomplished by going along
with the flow.

IMAGE

Wind traveling over water symbolizes dis-

persal. Kings of yore set up shrines to honor
God.

COMPONENTS

1 *yin*. It bodes well if the horse used for res-
cue is strong. *Image.* For the weak at the outset, good luck is a matter of following along.

2 *yang*. On dispersal, run to support, and regret vanishes. *Image.* Running to support on
dispersal means getting your wish.

3 *yin*. Disperse yourself, and there is no regret. *Image.* Dispersing yourself means the
will is set elsewhere.

4 *yin*. Dispersing a mob is very auspicious.
With dispersal there is gathering, but not as
ordinarily thought. *Image.* Dispersing a mob
is very auspicious, gloriously great.

5 *yang*. Making the great call reach every-
where in a diaspora, there is no blame if the
king remains in spite of dispersion. *Image.*
There is no blame if the king remains, because that is the proper position.

6 *yang*. Disperse the blood, go far away, and
there is no problem. *Image.* Dispersing the
blood means staying away from harm.

60. REGULATION

Regulation is successful, but it will not do to persist in painful regulation.

OVERALL JUDGMENT

Regulation is successful, because firmness and flexibility are proportionate, and firmness is centered. It will not do to persist in painful regulation, because that way leads to exhaustion. Passing through danger joyfully, fulfill your position in a regulated way, and master it with balance and uprightness. The four seasons take place by the regulation of heaven and earth. When measures are formulated in a regulated way, they do not damage property or harm the people.

IMAGE

There is water over a lake, symbolizing regulation. Cultured people formulate numbers and measures in consideration of virtuous behavior.

COMPONENTS

1 *yang.* There is no blame if you do not leave

133

the inner yard. *Image.* Not leaving the inner yard means knowing what will succeed and what will be thwarted.

2 *yang.* It is unlucky not to leave the outer yard. *Image.* What is unlucky about not leaving the outer yard is utterly missing timely opportunities.

3 *yin.* If you are not regulated, you will be sorry, but there is no one to blame. *Image.* When you are sorry because you are not regulated, who else is to blame?

4 *yin.* Stable regulation is successful. *Image.* Stable regulation succeeds insofar as it means taking up a higher course of action.

5 *yang.* Comfortable regulation bodes well; there is value in going on. *Image.* Comfortable regulation bodes well insofar as one is poised in centered balance.

6 *yin.* It bodes ill to persist in painful regulation, but regret vanishes. *Image.* It bodes ill to persist in painful regulation, because that leads to exhaustion.

61. TRUTHFULNESS IN THE CENTER

Truthfulness in the center is auspicious for the simpleminded. It is helpful for crossing great rivers. It is helpful to the upright.

OVERALL JUDGMENT

With truthfulness in the center, flexibility is within, and firm strength gains balance in the center. Joyous and harmonious, truthfulness thus civilizes the country. To say that it is auspicious for the simpleminded means that sincerity reaches even the simpleminded. It is helpful for crossing great rivers in that it is like riding on a boat that goes along with the flow unburdened. Helping the upright with truthfulness in the center is responding to the divine.

IMAGE

There is wind over a lake, representing truthfulness in the center. Cultured people make judgments with consideration and are lenient with the death sentence.

COMPONENTS

1 *yang.* Steady concentration bodes well; if
there is distraction, you are uneasy. *Image.*
For the strong at the outset, steady concentration bodes well; this means one's will has
not wavered.

2 *yang.* A calling crane is in the shade; its
fledgling joins it. When I have a fine goblet, I
will drink it up with you. *Image.* For one's
fledgling to join one is the wish at the core
of the heart.

3 *yin.* Finding opposition, you may drum or
you may stop, you may weep or you may
sing. *Image.* That you may drum or you may
stop means that your position is not managed correctly.

4 *yin.* With the moon almost full, the loss of
teammates is not blamed. *Image.* The loss of
teammates means parting with peers to rise
higher.

5 *yang.* To have truthfulness that is spellbinding is blameless. *Image.* To have truthfulness
that is spellbinding means that your position
is correctly managed.

6 *yang*. When a chicken tries to fly up into the skies, it bodes ill to persist. *Image.* When a chicken tries to fly up to the skies, how can it last?

62. PREDOMINANCE OF THE SMALL

When the small predominates, it gets through successfully, beneficial if correct. It is suitable for small matters, but not for great matters. The call left by a flying bird should not rise but descend; that is very auspicious.

OVERALL JUDGMENT

Predominance of the small means the small predominates and gets through successfully. Predominance that is beneficial to the correct is action in concert with the times. Flexibility is central; that is why it is auspicious for small matters. Strength is out of place and imbalanced, so it will not do for great matters. Therein is the image of a bird in flight; the sound left by the bird in flight should not go upward but downward. That would be very auspicious, because going upward would be going against the flow, while going downward would be going with the flow.

IMAGE

There is thunder over a mountain, symbolizing predominance of the small. Cultured people are extraordinarily reverential in their behavior, extraordinarily sorrowful in mourning, and extraordinarily frugal in their needs.

COMPONENTS

1 *yin.* A bird in flight is considered bad luck. *Image.* The ill omen represented by a bird in flight refers to something about which nothing can be done.

2 *yin.* When you have passed the grandmother but meet the mother, or when you cannot reach the ruler but meet the minister, there is no blame. *Image.* When you cannot reach the ruler, the minister cannot be passed over.

3 *yang.* It is foreboding when you may be attacked by pursuers if you are not exceedingly defensive against them. *Image.* Pursuers may attack you; that is unfortunate, but the question is what you can do about it.

4 *yang.* Impeccability is met if you do not go too far. When it is dangerous to go on, it is imperative to be cautious. Do not deliberately persist forever. *Image.* If you meet something on the condition that you do not go too far, this means you are out of place. When it is dangerous to go on, it is imperative to be cautious; after all it cannot continue forever.

5 *yin.* Dense clouds not raining come from one's own western province. A duke shoots and takes the quarry in its den. *Image.* Dense clouds not raining have already risen.

6 *yin.* Not meeting, going too far, the bad luck of the departure of a bird in flight; this is called trouble. *Image.* Not meeting and going too far refer to having gone too high.

63. ALREADY ACCOMPLISHED

The success of the already accomplished is at its minimum. It is beneficial if consistently correct. What starts out auspicious may end up a shambles.

OVERALL JUDGMENT

The success of that which is already accomplished is success at its minimum. It is beneficial if consistently correct, which means being firm and flexible in the right ways and in the right situations. A start that is auspicious is when flexibility is in balance; if that eventually stops, there is chaos, for the indicated path comes to an end.

IMAGE

Water is on top of fire, symbolizing the already accomplished. Cultured people give thought to troubles so as to prevent them by foresight.

COMPONENTS

1 *yang.* Drag your wheels, wet your tail, and

you won't have problems. *Image.* Drag your wheels, and it is logical that you won't have problems.

2 *yin.* When a woman loses her headdress, she should not chase after it; she will get it in seven days. *Image.* Getting it in seven days means taking a centered and balanced course.

3 *yang.* When an emperor attacks a devilish region, it takes three years to conquer it. Petty people are not to be employed. *Image.* Taking three years to conquer it means fatigue.

4 *yin.* With cloth wadding for leaks, be on the alert all day. *Image.* Being on the alert all day means there is something in doubt.

5 *yang.* The slaughtered ox of the neighbors to the east is not as good as the simple ceremony of the neighbors to the west, for really receiving the blessings. *Image.* The neighbors to the east, in slaughtering an ox, do not compare to the timing of the neighbors to the west. Really receiving the blessings is when good fortune comes in abundance.

6 *yin.* Getting the head wet is dangerous. *Image.* Getting the head wet is dangerous; how long can you last?

64. UNFINISHED

The unfinished being carried out is a small fox almost finished making a crossing; if it gets its head wet, nothing is profited.

OVERALL JUDGMENT

When the unfinished gets carried out, that means flexibility is balanced. A small fox almost finished making a crossing represents not having gone out of centered balance. If it gets its head wet, nothing is profited; this means not continuing to the end. This is a situation where firmness and flexibility correspond even though they are not in the right places.

IMAGE

Fire is above water, representing the unfinished. Cultured people use prudence to distinguish things and keep them in their places.

COMPONENTS

1 *yin.* It is embarrassing to get the tail wet. *Image.* Getting the tail wet means not even knowing your limits.

2 *yang.* Dragging the wheels, it bodes well to be steadfast and true. *Image.* For the strong in this position, steadfast truth that bodes well means acting correctly with centered balance.

3 *yin.* It bodes ill to go on before finishing, but it will be profitable to cross great rivers. *Image.* It bodes ill to go on before finishing, because the situation is not right.

4 *yang.* Integrity bodes well; regret will disappear. Stir into action to attack a devilish faction, and in three years be rewarded with a great country. *Image.* Integrity bodes well, for regret disappears; this is when an intention is put into effect.

5 *yin.* Integrity is auspicious; there is no regret. When there is truth in the brilliance of cultured people, that is auspicious. *Image.* The shining of the brilliance of cultured peo-

ple is auspicious.

6 *yang.* There is no blame in having faith in drinking wine, but if you souse your head it is no longer right to have faith. *Image.* To souse your head drinking wine means being immoderate.

NOTES

1. THE CREATIVE

Overall Judgment

"Clouds and rain" symbolize fecundity.

"Six stages"/"six dragons" refer to the six components of a hexagrammatic symbol.

"Dragon" symbolizes energy and power.

Components

The six components of The Creative are models for the process of spiritual alchemy known as "fostering the yang fire," which means developing energy. The general process illustrated by the six dragons may be taken to refer to any sort of undertaking or action, although it has a special inner meaning in the process of development and refinement of consciousness by spiritual alchemy. See *The Book of Balance and Harmony* (Berkeley, Calif.: North Point Press, 1989), "The Firing Process," pp. 104–105.

2. THE RECEPTIVE

"Chaste" means restrained, steadfast, true.

"Mare" symbolizes gentle, docile strength, yin power.

Components

The six lines of The Receptive are models for the process of moderating energy and achieving adaptable power under control. See *The Book of Balance and Harmony,* "The Firing Process," pp. 104–105.

5 yin: "Yellow" symbolizes the middle, the center, balance.

6 yin: "Battle in the fields" stands for "conquering inner demons." "Their blood is dusky yellow" means balance is blurred.

5. WAITING

"To cross great rivers" means to carry out major undertakings.

Components

6 yin: "Three unhurried guests" stand for the gradual rising of positive energy, represented by the first three yang components.

8. ACCORD

Components

1 yin: "Plain vessel" stands for a pure and simple heart and mind.

9. NURTURE OF THE SMALL

"Dense clouds not raining come from your own western region" symbolize energy building up gradually out of inner passivity, on the verge of bursting into action. The western direction is symbolically associated with the yin mode, which is also represented by smallness.

10. TREADING

To "tread on a tiger's tail" means to go through dangerous or delicate situations calling for great caution and tact.

11. TRANQUILLITY

Components

1 yang: "A reed" is a grass that grows from a continuous root, so reeds come in clusters when pulled out. This symbolizes the clustering or unification of the attention, loyalty, effort, or other resources of a group.

5 yin: "The emperor marries off his younger sister for good luck" symbolizes acting on aspirations in a balanced way, in that the marriage represents an alliance, which is both a combining and a sharing of power.

13. SAMENESS WITH PEOPLE

"Sameness with people in the wilds" symbolizes cooperation with others in a state of objective neediness and want.

Components

4 yang: "When you climb the walls but cannot attack successfully, that is lucky" in the sense that it is justice when aggression is unsuccessful.

5 yang: "First you weep, later you laugh: the great general conquers, then holds meetings"—Honesty may be painful at first, but once it is established, good relations can develop.

15. HUMILITY

Components

1 yin: "Humbly humble" means humility without self-consciousness or artificiality.

4 yin: To "disperse humility" means to apply humility to all aspects of life.

17. FOLLOWING

Components

1 yang: "Outside the gate" represents public life.

2 yin: "Child/adult" stand for lesser and greater concerns or occupations.

19. OVERSEEING

"The eighth month" stands for the waning of positive energy.

21. BITING THROUGH

"Biting through" means cutting through difficulties.

Components

6 yang: A "cangue" is a large wooden square locked around the neck as punishment.

22. ADORNMENT

Components

5 yin: "For adornment in the hills and gardens, a bolt of silk is too small. It is embarrassing, but the end is lucky." Simplicity and minimalism may seem unbecoming to people in high positions, but the results are good.

23. STRIPPING AWAY

Components

5 yin: "A string of fish" refers to the first through fourth yin components of this sign, symbolizing a group of humble people.

25. FIDELITY

Components

3 yin: "The misfortune of fidelity" means clinging to harmful fixations.

29. CONSTANT PITFALLS

Components

4 yin: "Use a plain cup" means be without artificiality. "A pledge through a window" symbolizes communication with openness and clarity.

30. FIRE

Components

6 yang: "The captives are not of the same kind, so they are not blamed." Only the leaders of a mob are targeted in a punitive action; the masses of followers are controlled by outside forces, so they are not of the same kind as instigators and leaders.

31. SENSITIVITY

Components

2 yin: "Sensing the calf unlucky, it would be lucky to stay put." The calf must follow the direction of the foot if the leg is to move: if the foot turns in a wrong direction but the calf does not follow, the leg will not proceed in that way. This is the function of secondary conscience and self-examination.

3 yang: "It is embarrassing to go on" in the sense that it is lowly to be other-directed and not autonomous.

6 yin: "Speaking with the mouth up close" in reference to matters so sensitive that they are spoken of in whispers.

32. PERSISTENCE

Components

5 yin: Here "woman" means yin in the sense of

single-minded devotion, while "man" means yang in the sense of multifaceted attention. Both exist in each individual person, but are most effective when used in the respectively appropriate places at the right times.

34. THE POWER OF GREATNESS

Components

1 yang: "When the power is in the feet" means when the motive force is impulsive; in such cases "certainty will wear out" when emotion abates.

5 yin: "Losing the ram in ease" means losing energy by becoming complacent.

35. ADVANCE

"A secure lord uses gift horses in abundance" — A stable leader who does not monopolize power and its perquisites grows in strength by sharing with others.

Components

2 yin: "Grandmother" stands for the 5 yin component of this hexagram.

4 yang: "Like a squirrel" means erratic and inconstant, as if hopping from branch to branch.

6 yang: "Advancing the horns is only used for conquering the heartland" — Aggressive corrective action should be directed only toward oneself or one's own domain of activity, according to an-

cient humanistic philosophies like Taoism and original Confucianism, insofar as it is impossible to correct others without self-correction. It is further believed that massive force would not be needed in a perfectly just action, because the charisma of true justice would enter into the dynamics of the entire situation.

39. HALTING

For halting, the southwest is advantageous, not the northeast. The southwest direction is associated with the qualities of receptivity and harmony, being still and open; the northwest is associated with arrest and vitiation of energy. The point is that when halting at obstacles, it is beneficial to remain in a state of alert poise, and not fall into numb passivity or inhibition; only thus will it be possible to get past obstacles and resolve halting.

40. SOLUTION

For "there is profit in the southwest," see note to hexagram 39.

Components

2 yang: "Three foxes" stand for the three yin components above this one in the hexagram; "catching three foxes" means leading those of higher rank but lesser ability.

4 yang: When you "remove your big toe" means
when you are not vehement or aggressive.

41. REDUCTION

The "two bowls" represent yang and yin modes:
filling and emptying, activity and passivity.

Components

5 yin: "ten pairs of tortoises" Tortoises were very
valuable for both their flesh and their shells; ten
pairs could also be used to breed and provide a
self-renewing source of wealth. Therefore ten
pairs of tortoises represents rich resources, help
from above.

42. INCREASE

Components

2 yin: For "ten pairs of tortoises," see note to
hexagram 41.

"It is auspicious for the king to purposefully
make offerings to God." Those who are successful should be grateful for the help they receive,
and refrain from attributing their success to
themselves alone; this is auspicious for them because they may thereby avoid potentially cata-
strophic conceit and complacency.

43. DECISIVENESS

Components

3 yang: "Vigor in the face" means a show of emotion.

44. MEETING
Components
1 yin: An "emaciated pig" symbolizes someone in desperation.

46. RISING
"An expedition south bodes well." The southern direction is associated with fire, which symbolizes perceptivity, awareness, and intelligence.
Components
2 yang: "Using ceremony" means being courteous.

47. EXHAUSTION
Components
2 yang: The "regal garment" symbolizes ennoblement.
4 yang: "Gold" symbolizes the yang mode.

49. CHANGE
Components
1 yang: To "use the hide of a yellow ox" means to be firm, centered, and taciturn.

50. THE CAULDRON
Components
1 yin: "When one takes a concubine, as long as she has a son there is no blame." When measures

of secondary resort are taken, if they in fact accomplish the required task, then they are considered good enough.

3 yang: "Pheasant fat" stands for rich food, high living.

"Just when it rains" means when yang is tempered by yin.

5 yin: Here "gold" symbolizes centered balance (from the association of its yellow color), while "jade" symbolizes flexibility and coolness.

6 yang: A "jade handle" stands for yin; a yin image in a yang component stands for the combination of yin and yang, which is the Way: therefore this combination is very auspicious, beneficial all around.

51. THUNDER

Components

2 yin: "you climb up nine hills" The number 9 symbolizes yang, particularly mature yang; here, "climbing up nine hills" stands for yin seeking yang.

"you will get it in seven days" The number 7 symbolizes young yang; it also stands for 6 + 1, which means the next phase of development to take place after what is indicated by the six components of the present hexagram.

55. ABUNDANCE

Components

2 yin: When "you see the north star in the daytime," this means there is darkness when there should be light.

3 yang: When "you see droplets in the sun," this means there is a diffusion of light.

56. TRAVEL

Components

3 yang: "If you burn the inn and lose your servants. . . ."—If you are destructively careless with material and human resources. . . .

5 yin: "Shooting at a pheasant, one arrow is lost." Sacrifice may be necessary for the attainment of an aim.

62. PREDOMINANCE OF THE SMALL

Components

2 yin:	grandmother	here stands for 1 yin
	mother	here stands for 5 yin
	ruler	here stands for 5 yin
	minister	here stands for 4 yang

The qualities of the second component should combine with those of the fifth, by virtue of position, but if the level of the fifth component is not reached, 2 yin and 4 yang may combine by virtue of complementarity of qualities.

5 yin: The "duke" symbolizes the fifth component, which represents leadership. To "take the quarry in its den" means to take care of things while they are still small or subtle.

63. ALREADY ACCOMPLISHED

Components

1 yang: "Drag your wheels, wet your tail" — Slow down and stop.

2 yin: The "woman's headdress" refers to the yang complement of yin; here it specifically means the complementary component 5 yang.

6 yin: "Getting the head wet" means getting too deeply immersed.

List of Hexagrams
with
Their Primal
Correlates
and
Structural
Complements

List of Hexagrams with Their Primal Correlates and Structural Complements

HEXAGRAM	CORRELATE	COMPLEMENT
1. The Creative	2. The Receptive	2. The Receptive
2. The Receptive	1. The Creative	1. The Creative
3. Difficulty	20. Observing	50. The Cauldron
4. Innocence	19. Overseeing	49. Change
5. Waiting	57. Conformity	35. Advance
6. Contention	58. Pleasing	36. Injury to the Enlightened
7. An Army	13. Sameness with People	13. Sameness with People
8. Accord	27. Nourishment	14. Great Possession
9. Nurture of the Small	32. Persistence	16. Happiness

Consultation Chart

TRIGRAMS			
UPPER ♦	☰	☱	☳
LOWER ♦	Sky	Lake	Thunder
☰ Sky	1	43	34
☱ Lake	10	58	54
☳ Thunder	25	17	51
☲ Fire	13	49	55
☷ Earth	12	45	16
☶ Mountain	33	31	62
☵ Water	6	47	40
☴ Wind	44	28	32

☲	☷	☶	☵	☴
Fire	Earth	Mountain	Water	Wind
14	11	26	5	9
38	19	41	60	61
21	24	27	3	42
30	36	22	63	37
35	2	23	8	20
56	15	52	39	53
64	7	4	29	59
50	46	18	48	57

LIBRARY OF CONGRESS
CATALOGING-IN-PUBLICATION DATA

I Ching / translated by Thomas Cleary. — 1st ed.
        p.   cm. — (Shambhala pocket classics)
    ISBN 0-87773-661-8 (pbk.: alk. paper)
1. I ching.   I. Cleary, Thomas F., 1949–   .   II. Series.
        PL2464.Z6I14   1992   91-53089
        299'.51282—dc20   CIP